THINK
PROGRESS

ALSO BY SKIP J. WILLIAMS
Think & Win Big

SKIP J. WILLIAMS

THINK
PROGRESS
Creative. Innovative. Solutions.

PIKS BOOKS

Piks Books, a division of Skip Williams Communications LLC, New York

Piks Books may be ordered via booksellers and purchased in bulk for educational, business, fund-raising, or sales promotional use. For information, please e-mail piksinfo@skipwilliamsonline.com

Think Progress: Innovative. Creative. Solutions.
ISBN 978-0-9839818-2-4 (2012 edition / paperback)
ISBN 978-0-9839818-3-1 (2012 edition / ebook)

Printed in the United States of America

Second Edition

This book is dedicated to my two personal cheerleaders:

Mrs. Minnie "Gorgeous" Ellington
&
Mother Hicks

Thank you for the endless love, prayers, support,
and words of wisdom. I needed each and every
one of them...literally!

I LOVE YOU

CONTENTS

*"A closed-mind will walk
into the I <u>can't</u> walls.
An open-mind will find and run
through the I <u>can</u> doors."*
–SKIP J. WILLIAMS

1

IDEAS MAKE THE WORLD GO AROUND

"We are what we think.
All that we are arises with our thoughts.
With our thoughts, we make the world."
–BUDDHA

Before we begin, I would like for you to take a deep breath. Exhale. Now, take a look around you. What do you see? Every day we see them. Hear them. Touch them. Smell them. Taste them. We even buy, sell, and use them. What are they? They are called *ideas*.

Everywhere we go there is at least one idea in the vicinity. Have you ever thought about where all of the products and services that you use come from? Or who developed them? Yes, we have seen the amusing insurance commercials advertising their services on television. Yes, we have noticed the new movies that will be in theaters this weekend. Yes, we have heard about the retail stores that will be having sales this week. Although there are countless products and services around us, each one of them was created by individuals and a collaboration of *ideas*.

As Ted Joans once stated, "Everything that is was once imagined." There are over 6 billion people throughout the world, which means there are billions of ideas conceived every second. For instance, the clothes we wear to our favorite songs all the way to the new feature on our cell phones–were all created from ideas. Likewise, if you work for a company or have your own company it was launched from an idea. Everything that has reached success started from an *idea*.

Though companies create and sell their ideas every day, they continue to seek innovative ways to improve their brands. For example, when companies have their daily and/or weekly meetings, everyone is asked to put in his or her input (ideas) to improve the quality of the products,

1

services, and company. Also, some companies provide "suggestion boxes" for their employees and customers to submit new ideas. One reason a few companies use the *suggestion box* method is because they know every person has an idea; however, some people would like to share their ideas and stay anonymous.

SMALL IDEAS COUNT TOO

Successful people are creative thinkers. Their minds are constantly in "think" mode, as they look for golden opportunities to develop their ideas into success. In 1893, William Wrigley Jr. started selling *Wrigley's Juicy Fruit and Wrigley's Spearmint* chewing gum, which he sold both for under a dollar. Today, Wrigley's is a billion dollar company, as they continue to sell their 5 sticks pack of *Spearmint and Juicy Fruit* chewing gum for less than 50 cents.

The French poet and novelist, Victor Hugo once said, "Nothing can stop an idea whose time has come." Everything starts with an idea. You can have a big or a small idea and succeed. It's not the *size* of your ideas that will display your success. It's what you *do* with your ideas that will make your ideas grow into a success.

THE CREATIVE GENIUS

There is a *genius* within you. As a progress thinker, you don't have to wait for others to label you as a "genius." Neither do you have to appear on the front cover of every publication throughout the universe to be considered successful.

In 1982, Dave Gold, the founder of the 99¢ Only Stores, opened the doors to his first store. Inside of his new establishment, he sold every item for only 99 cents. Today, Dave Gold has done more than expanded his 99¢ Only Stores from California, Texas, Arizona and Nevada, he has built his company into a multi-million dollar empire, simply by using his creativity.

What made Dave Gold's company stand out from the competition? His creativity. While other companies decided to work super hard, Dave decided to work super creative. If you noticed in Dave Gold's case, sometimes it's good to think smaller.

All of us have unlimited creativity within us. While many people choose to work hard to succeed. The creative thinkers choose to work creatively to succeed. Creative thinkers are constantly seeking new ideas and elite resources that will enable them to succeed and stand out from the crowd. For example, there are thousands of products displayed and marketed via TV, magazines, billboards, and radio. Among all of the products, the ones that stand out the most are usually the products with a humorous, creative and unique twist to them.

As a progress thinker, you don't have to wait or depend on others to call you a "genius." What if no one calls you a "genius?" Then what? You don't have to be the brightest crayon in the box to become a creative genius. When it comes to creativity, you don't have to be the smartest person in the world to be called a "genius." All you need is an idea that is creative. Once you have a creative idea, apply physical action toward your idea. The more action you take toward your ideas, the more you will stand out like a creative genius.

HELP OTHERS SUCCEED

On various occasions people ask me, "What is the secret to success?" One of the best ways to succeed is to *help others*. Zig Ziglar, the motivational speaker and author, declared, "You can get everything in life you want if you help enough people get what they want." When you help *others* succeed, they will help *you* succeed.

Every person on earth has ideas. However, everyone doesn't know what to do with his or her own ideas. Some people let their ideas mentally collect dust by not taking action toward their ideas. Others choose to take advantage of their ideas and succeed. When you have an idea, do something with your idea. Seek creative and profitable ways to share your idea with others. This simple and effective strategy will do more than help you make progress; it will enable you to succeed faster.

Successful people and companies are always seeking innovative avenues that will give them the opportunity to display their ideas for others to see, purchase and use. When you have ideas, share your ideas. Don't be afraid to reveal and present your ideas with confidence. The key is to share your ideas with more people. Once you do, more people will show you how much they appreciate your ideas by purchasing and requesting more of your product or services.

What idea(s) do you have–past or present–that will help someone else besides yourself succeed? Rather than thinking with a "What's in it for *me?*" mentality, start thinking with a "What can I do for *others?*" and "How can I *share* my idea?" mentality. As Deion Sanders a.k.a. "Primetime" stated during his 2011 *NFL Hall of Fame* induction speech, "If your dream is not bigger than yourself there's something wrong with your dream." There is nothing wrong with dreaming; however, successful people dream bigger than themselves. As a progress thinker, keep in mind the more people that *you* help succeed; the more they will help you succeed.

When it comes to helping others, you don't have to reinvent the wheel to succeed. You can implement what David Kord Murray calls "borrowing brilliance." In his book *Borrowing Brilliance*, David Kord Murray describes how numerous successful people and companies have creatively borrowed the ideas of others and used them to succeed. As David Kord Murray affirmed, "It's an evolutionary thing that makes use of previous ideas to give birth to new ones."

If you notice, your idea could simply be an extension of an idea that already exists. For instance, you could take an original idea, add your own twist, flavor or vision to it, then make it your own innovative idea. This simple formula happens every day. Think about it. How many different cars do you see on the road? How many cellular phones and phone plans do you hear about? How many websites do you come across on the Internet? Every car, cellular phone and website is equipped with multiple features. Why? Because the various features (ideas) make each one of them unique and we are habitually attracted to new and improved products and services.

Borrowing brilliance will enhance your opportunities to become brilliant too. This technique is also called, "modeling." In short term, *modeling* is duplicating what works. For example, if you noticed that something worked successfully, simply *model* the successful person, company, product or service. In other words, do the same thing that successful people do to succeed. When you do what works, you will begin to produce successful results.

THE VALUE OF IDEAS

The author Napoleon Hill, once stated, "Ideas are the beginning points to all fortunes." Your ideas are valuable; don't waste them. Every one of your ideas won't make you an instant millionaire or billionaire; however, over time your ideas could make you wealthy. The thought may enter your mind, "Nobody wants my ideas." From my personal experience, I can truly say, "Yes, someone wants and needs your ideas." There is always a recipient for your ideas.

There were times in my life when numerous people literally told me, "No one wants your ideas." After hearing that phrase over and over again, I could have listened to them, folded up my tent and rode off into the sunset feeling defeated. However, I believed in myself enough to look passed the negativity that was thrown at me. What did I do? Instead of walking around with my head down, I lifted my head up and pushed forward. One idea that I had was to write and publish a book. As you continue to read *Think Progress*, you are reading one of my ideas that naysayers told me that nobody would want.

> "Everyone who's ever taken a shower
> has an idea. It's the person who gets out of
> the shower, dries off, and does something about it
> who makes the differences."
> –NOLAN BUSHNELL

Some people will try to talk you out of your own ideas by calling you "crazy," "weird," and "a dreamer." They will also tell you, "It will never work." Don't fall into their negative trap. When you have an idea, you must believe in your idea enough to take action toward it. Nolan Bushnell, the founder of *Atari, Pong* and *Chuck E. Cheese's Pizza*, was correct when he said, "Everyone who's ever taken a shower has an idea. It's the person who gets out of the shower, dries off, and does something about it who makes the differences."

Just because someone utters, "You can't succeed" doesn't mean you have to listen to or believe the person. Every idea has the potential to create something valuable, even the ones that naysayers think no one wants. Others may not see, understand or believe in your ideas, but that's why it's vital that you believe in yourself and your ideas. Your ideas are valuable assets, which means your ideas are too valuable to waste. If you refuse to follow through on your ideas, it may cost you a fortune financially, mentally, emotionally and physically. You can achieve your ideas, when you take action toward them. The more action you take toward your ideas, the more opportunities you will receive to transform your ideas into success. If I succeeded, so can you. When you believe in yourself and your ideas, keep moving forward until you achieve your goals.

A DELICIOUS IDEA

When Debbi Fields first launched her company in 1977, she opened her first store in Palo Alto, California. Debbi called her newfound store *Mrs. Fields,* where she sold cookies. Yes, there were naysayers who told Debbi that her business would fail, but she disregarded their negative comments and succeeded anyway. Debbi Fields had an idea just like you and I. There is one key distinction that enabled Debbi to prevail: Not only did she take action toward her idea, but Debbi also followed through until she achieved her goal. Today, the *Mrs. Fields* company has expanded worldwide, as millions of taste buds from all over the world continue to enjoy her delicious cookies.

When ideas enter your mind don't sit on them by thinking no one wants them. There is an array of people who "want" and "need" your ideas. New ideas are constantly *wanted* and *needed* every single day. An effective way to make progress is to present your ideas for others to see and use them. An abundance of ideas are ready to blossom within you. Take the lid off your mental cookie jar and start implementing your ideas today.

THE DOOR TO OPPORTUNITY IS ALWAYS OPEN

In the Bible, (Matthew 7:7) it says, "Ask and it shall be given to you; seek and ye shall find; knock and it shall be opened unto you." At work, it's called "the open door policy." In life, it's called "the open door to opportunities."

When new opportunities present themselves to you there is no need to fear or run from them. An *opportunity* is like a door with your name on it. As you stand at the door, with your name on it, what will you do? Will you <u>open</u> the door and *walk through it*? Or will you keep your door <u>closed</u>, turn around, and *walk away from it*? When opportunities knock on your door welcome and accept them with open arms.

The mind is filled with *ideas* like each moment is filled with *opportunities*. There are countless opportunities around us at all times. Some of us see the opportunities. While a few of us overlook the opportunities. One reason a lot of people overlook the opportunities around them is because they refuse to open their minds to new ideas. It's the new ideas that create the new opportunities. On the contrary, it's the new opportunities that create the new ideas. Most successful people see opportunities around them because they are open-minded. If you observed the high achievers that make the most progress in their careers, finances, and relationships you would discover the majority of them are open-minded.

> *"If you want to succeed in the world,*
> *you must make your own opportunities."*
> –JOHN B. GOUGH

John B. Gough, author and temperance orator, once said, "If you want to succeed in the world, you must make your own opportunities." As human beings, we are the gatekeepers to our own personal success. Every person, including you, has a set of master keys that will unlock the doors on his or her own success path. The manner, in which we choose to use our minds will either *open* or *close* the doors to our personal success.

Progress starts with an open mind. The next time you need to make a decision will you have an "open" or "closed" mindset? Having a *closed-mind* is equivalent to looking at a blank movie screen. In other words, nothing takes place when the mind is closed. When you "close" your mind you will keep yourself from seeing the opportunities. When you "open" your mind you will allow yourself to see more opportunities that will enable you to succeed. To advance in life you must be willing to open your mind to new concepts. When you become open-minded, you will begin to see and enter the doors that will lead you to the next level personally and professionally.

UNEMPLOYED TO ENTREPRENEUR

Before I started my own company, Skip Williams Communications, I worked at several 9-to-5 jobs. A few of the jobs laid me off, but I never cried foul or never viewed it from a negative point of view. I just took all of my previous work experiences and used them to my advantage. While unemployed, I was eligible to collect unemployment benefits. One day as I was looking at the small amount on my unemployment checks I literally told myself, "There must be a better way and I'm going to find it."

One afternoon while I was still unemployed, I received a letter from the Department of Labor notifying me that I had to visit my local Department of Labor office in-person. The letter also stated that I needed to bring in the document that was attached to the letter. The document was a log sheet for me to list all the attempts I had made in searching for a job.

Approximately two weeks later, the day arrived when I had to report to the Department of Labor office. The Department of Labor representative asked to see my log sheet, which I presented to her. After briefly looking at my log sheet, she noticed it was blank. She said, "Mr. Williams do you know what this log sheet is for?" I said, "Yes Ma'am." She said, "Do you know how to use the log sheet?" I said, "Yes Ma'am." Then she asked me the million-dollar question: "So, why didn't you write anything down on your log sheet?"

With confidence in my voice I replied, "I am an entrepreneur!" The representative looked at me in a dumbfounded manner. As I continued to answer her question, I said, "The reason I didn't write anything down on the log sheet is because I've decided to start my own company." The representative was speechless as she pulled her eyeglasses off and placed them on her desk. In conclusion, I politely declared to the representative, "I never want to be put in this situation again, collecting an unemployment check."

That was my defining moment. That was the moment I received my internal wake-up call. I knew it was time for me to stand up and take charge of my life. It was during my setback of being unemployed that I made the ultimate decision to start thinking progress. Being unemployed compelled me to think bigger and it made me think more creatively. Being unemployed inadvertently forced me to take the necessary risks to start my own company.

As a progress thinker, I have too many ideas and big dreams that I want to accomplish and I refuse to waste my time, dreams and ideas on not achieving them. This is one of the main reasons why I wake up early and stay up late, because I am constantly in pursuit of achieving more of my dreams. When I was unemployed, I believed in my ideas and I believed in myself enough to launch my own company. As the proud owner of Skip Williams Communications, I can honestly say that I'm happy with the decision and actions that I made to venture out as an entrepreneur. Today, I am still having fun and taking the action steps toward my own ideas and big dreams every single day.

One major lesson I learned while being unemployed: When you have a talent and you've discovered your talent, don't waste your talent–do something with your talent. As a progress thinker, it doesn't matter if you're an employee, an employer, or unemployed–you are always the Founder, President and CEO of your own dreams, life and success.

FROM AN ENTREPRENEURIAL POINT OF VIEW

We have all heard and read the stories about companies downsizing, leaving thousands of men and women unemployed. In the midst of being downsized, countless people are looking for new jobs via surfing the Internet, flipping through their local newspapers, and physically submitting their resumes in-person to various companies. While many unemployed people have chosen to go the traditional route and seek employment, a few people who were once unemployed have chosen to take a different route by viewing the downsizing as the perfect opportunity to start their own businesses. They chose to take advantage of their own ideas and have decided to become *entrepreneurs*.

Entrepreneurs have discovered the value of having their own ideas. One secret about entrepreneurs: They don't enjoy seeing their ideas wasted, put on the back burner or sitting on someone else's shelf collecting dust on top of them. Rather than wasting or throwing away their ideas, entrepreneurs seek innovative and profitable ways to utilize their own ideas productively. This explains why more college students, parents, and creative individuals are starting to launch their own home-based Internet businesses, instead of waiting for someone else to start a company just to hire and fire them. Today, more entrepreneurs are taking their ideas into their own hands and turning them into success. Why?

Because as an entrepreneur opportunities are endless. As an entrepreneur, you have the opportunity to create your own paths, job and success.

As a progress thinker, start taking your ideas to the next level–from *mentally* thinking about them to *physically* achieving them. Remember, you can launch your own company with your own ideas. You never know, as an entrepreneur, your ideas may become the next trendsetter.

THE MONOPOLY OF IDEAS

There is a renowned phrase that says, "Money makes the world go around." That's partially correct. It's really the "ideas" of people that make the world go around.

In 1933, Charles Darrow created a small board game that featured various luxury streets in the vicinity of Atlantic City. The following street names are just a few that Mr. Darrow selected for his board game: Boardwalk, Park Place, and Baltic Avenue. The board game was named *Monopoly*. Charles Darrow created the *Monopoly* game from an idea. *Monopoly* continues to be a favorite board game played all over the world and has been translated into 43 languages.

There are millions of people who travel to Atlantic City and Las Vegas annually to spend their money inside the casinos. Every game inside of the casinos–from Blackjack to the slot machines– were all created from ideas. Though thousands of people have profited a lot of money playing the games inside the casinos, they are spending their money on ideas. We don't spend our money *on money*. We spend our money *on ideas*, which accumulates into money. For example, there are investors who invest their money on stocks and real estate because they want to enhance their wealth. When it comes to investments, what investors are really investing their money into are *ideas*–products, services and companies–that has the potential to multiply their wealth.

Wealthy people use the phrase "Make your *money* work for you." The same philosophy can be applied to your ideas: Make your *ideas* work for you. Your ideas are worth a fortune. Start investing in your own ideas. Once you start planting the seeds to your unique ideas, your ideas and wealth will begin to grow abundantly.

IT ONLY TAKES ONE

Mark Cuban, the owner of the NBA *Dallas Mavericks*, declared, "In business, to be a success, you only have to be right once. One single solitary time and you are set for life." Every millionaire and billionaire had to start somewhere before they reached success. Successful men and women build their success from their own ideas, which enables them to build their own wealth.

> *"In business, to be a success, you only have to be right once. One single solitary time and you are set for life."*
> –MARK CUBAN

Your success is only an idea away. It's what you mentally and physically do with your ideas that will produce your success. The following entrepreneurs succeeded by building on top of their ideas: Michael Dell, the founder of *Dell* computers, launched his company by building personal computers. Bill Gates and Paul Allen established *Microsoft* by creating software. Bobbi Brown started her *Bobbi Brown Cosmetic* brand with lipstick. Robert L. Johnson launched an innovative television network called *BET* (Black Entertainment Television). Howard Schultz took coffee to the next level by expanding *Starbucks* coffee worldwide. Jeff Hawkins, Donna Dubinsky and Ed Colligan developed their *Palm* company by inventing the *PalmPilot*. Mark Zuckerberg and his Harvard University classmates created their social network company called *Facebook*.

When it comes to success, the list is endless with successful people who started with just one product and service. The secret to having a successful idea is to implement your idea. Seek effective and profitable ways to build on top of your ideas.

Your *ideas* are valuable assets. You can build your own success and wealth with your ideas. When it comes to your ideas, you have a choice to either keep them to yourself or share them with others. The choice is yours. The latter – sharing your ideas with others – will present you with immeasurable pleasure, wealth and success. Remember, *one* idea could launch your success. Finish the following sentence with your own words: "If I had <u>one</u> idea it would be…" Write down your ideas. Review and focus on your ideas. Take physical action toward your ideas.

THINK PROGRESS

As a progress thinker, the more you *share* and/or *sell* your ideas, the more opportunities you will create for yourself to succeed. Keep in mind it's what you *do* with your ideas that will make the ultimate difference in your progress and success.

WRITE DOWN YOUR IDEAS

Everywhere I go I carry with me a mini notepad and a pen. I never leave home without them. My pen and mini notepad allow me to instantly write down my ideas. It may be a little old school, as some like to call it; however, I've used this concept for years. Whenever I have an idea, I write them down inside my mini notepad. It has become a natural and rewarding habit for me.

The author William Zinsser said, "Writing is thinking on paper." You never know when an idea may appear in your mind. This is one reason why it's important to be prepared for your forthcoming ideas by simply carrying a pen and mini notepad with you. Having a pen and mini notepad on hand is great because when you don't have access to your laptop and desktop computer, or when the battery on your Smartphone runs low, you will at least have your pen and mini notepad present to jot down your ideas.

Did you write down your ideas today? One effective way to succeed is to write down your ideas. You can buy a *single* or a *pack* of 3 x 5 mini notepads and a box of blue or black pens at your local office supply store. You will make more progress once you start writing down your ideas. When ideas enter your mind, simply write them down. Writing down your ideas will do more than enable you to unleash your mental creativity; it will also make more room for you to mentally create new ideas. Moreover, writing down your ideas will help you remember them. After writing down and reviewing your ideas, select your best ideas and start taking action to achieve them. The more action that you take toward your ideas, the more you will enhance the momentum to achieve them.

LET THE WORLD KNOW WHAT YOU ARE THINKING

You can have a ton of money. You can have the most degrees. You can even drive the most expensive and nicest car on earth. But, it will be your *ideas* that will let people know that you exist. You have thousands of ideas, what will you do with your ideas?

Let the world know what you are thinking. When you have ideas, don't waste them. Seek productive ways to share your ideas with others. At the end, you will be glad you did. When you share your ideas to help others, you will do more than discover your purpose, you will begin to add value and make the world a better place.

2

BUILD A STRONG
INTERNAL FOUNDATION

*"Put yourself in a state of mind where you say to
yourself, here is an opportunity for me to celebrate like
never before, my own power, my own ability
to get myself to do whatever is necessary."*
–ANTHONY ROBBINS

Building an *internal foundation* will be the next step to making successful progress. At the beginning of every building, house, business, and person there is a layer called the *foundation*.

What is a foundation? A foundation is the first layer to building a successful establishment. Your *body* is your establishment. Your *mind* is your foundation. The internal foundation is where everything begins. We create who we are by the thoughts that we develop inside our minds. Are you envisioning *positive* or *negative* pictures inside your mind? Do you imagine yourself *succeeding* or *failing*? As the architect of your life are you designing a *weak* or a *strong* foundation?

The strength of your *internal foundation* will be the starting point to creating your external success. Having a positive mental attitude, optimistic self-image, self-confidence, and self-acceptance are key elements that will enhance your internal base, progress and success. When you build a strong internal foundation, you will establish a well-built external foundation.

WHAT ARE YOU FEEDING YOUR MIND?

When you start your day, what is the *first* thought that enters your mind? Are your first thoughts *positive* or *negative*? Are your first thoughts *self-*

triumph or *self-defeat*? When I asked the previous question at one of my seminars, more than half of the audience raised their hands acknowledging that their first thoughts in the morning were negative and self-defeating. Rather than starting their day with positive words like, "Today is going to be a great day," many began their day with the phrase, "Oh no, not another one."

Most people think their breakfast begins in the morning with cereal, toast, pancakes, eggs, coffee, milk or orange juice. Yes, those are all forms of breakfast. However, our *mental breakfast* starts with our first thought upon waking up. What kind of breakfast are you feeding your mind every day? If you are waking up every morning and saying, "Oh no, not another one" – you are habitually injecting negative and unhealthy thoughts into your mind.

Yes, we all know there are 365 days in a year. However, if you are constantly feeding your mind with negative beliefs and visualizing yourself failing and/or losing, on a daily basis – that is 365 days of negative food entering your mind. Think about it. Three meals per day, plus snacks–that's a lot of negative mental food entering one mind. When you feed your mind with negativity, not only are you sabotaging yourself, you're also preparing yourself to be defeated.

Feeding your mind with negativity will do more than make you think negative. It will place a damper on your emotional pattern, which will limit your mental creativity and achievements, plus cause you to have a self-defeating day before you exit your home. Is that how you want to live your life on a daily basis? I hope not, because there are better ways to live and enjoy your life.

Don't defeat yourself before you start your day. Start your day by feeding your mind with *positive food*. When you wake up, get in the habit of telling yourself, "Today is going to be an outstanding day." Your mind needs to hear the positive voice *inside* of you, in order to produce positive results *outside* of you. Start feeding your mind with optimistic thoughts. The more you feed your mind with positive thoughts and visions, the more you will condition yourself to have a productive and prosperous day.

THE CONSEQUENCES OF LISTENING TO NEGATIVITY

Ever since Danny was a little boy, he dreamed about playing professional football. Wherever Danny went he talked about playing football. The more he talked about playing professional football, the more people uttered the negative words, "Dan, you're not going to make it as a professional football player."

As time went on Danny started allowing his mind to slowly absorb the negativity from others. His dreams of becoming a professional football player withered into a *"what if..."* Today, Danny reminisces about *what if* he would have believed in himself more and worked harder to become a NFL player? There are hundreds of professional football players. Why did Danny think he couldn't make it into the NFL? The answer: *Negative thinking.* Negative thinking led his mind and actions toward self-defeat. Danny *mentally* defeated himself.

Many people think others defeat them; however, some people defeat themselves. If Danny had believed in himself, he would have enhanced his chances of becoming a professional football player. Danny could have fulfilled his dreams, but he allowed the negative comments from the naysayers entertain his mind with negative thoughts. If you notice, thinking negative can make you *defeat* yourself, even when there is no competition in the vicinity. There is nothing enjoyable, great, adventurous, or rewarding about having a negative state of mind.

> *"No one can make you feel inferior without your consent."*
> –ELEANOR ROOSEVELT

The author Eleanor Roosevelt wrote, "No can make you feel inferior without your consent." In fact, your brain will only absorb whatever you want and allow it to soak in. At every moment of your life you have complete access to every thought that enters your mind – positive or negative, good or bad, right or left, forward or backward, on or off. What will you allow your mind to absorb today?

Most people think failure comes from procrastination, lack of education or money, and making mistakes. That's not always the case. Sometimes failure comes from thinking negative. How many negative thinkers do you know? I think all of us know at least one or a few negative thinkers. Just because others think negative that doesn't mean you have to think negative too. *Negative thinking will lead you to failure; positive thinking will lead you to success.* Please reread the previous sentence.

Negative thinkers refuse to think positive. Positive thinkers refuse to think negative. Don't let what happened to Danny happen to you. You have a dream–thrive to fulfill your dream. Your mind is too valuable to think negative. To become a strong person *physically*, you first must become a strong person *mentally*. As a progress thinker, you must be willing to condition your mind to think in an optimistic manner. Since you have to think anyway, why not think positive? One way to advance your progress is by conditioning your mind to think in a positive manner. When you think positive you will achieve your dreams.

THE OPEN AND OPTIMISTIC MIND

An *open* and *optimistic* mind is a grand and growing mind. If you want to impress someone, all you need to do is have an "open and optimistic" mindset. This is the best-kept secret to every success.

If you go through life with a closed and pessimistic mindset, how successful do you think you will become? Having a *closed-mind* will lead you to closed doors. Having an *open-mind* will lead you to open doors. You will encounter a few closed doors on your journey. This is why it's vital to have an open and optimistic mindset, because when you have an open mind you will begin to see the paths that will lead you to open doors.

Progress and success starts with an open and optimistic mindset. Progress thinkers succeed because they are optimistic and open-minded. Most of the successful decision makers throughout the world are open-minded and optimistic thinkers. Their minds are always open, as they seek innovative ways to create and discover new opportunities to prevail.

When it comes to making effective decisions in your life, having an open and optimistic mind is a necessity to succeed. When you think with an open and optimistic mindset it will enable you to display your mental and physical creativity.

3

THE PROCESS OF PROGRESS

"Progress is the beauty of success."
–SKIP J. WILLIAMS

When your objective is to succeed, you will first need to start the *process* to create a momentum toward what you want to achieve. It will be the "process" stage that will enable you to make progress. Nothing gets accomplished without going through a process. For example, a closed door won't open until someone makes an effort to open it. Success is the same way. The door to your success will remain closed until you make the effort to open it.

Before Babe Ruth and Hank Aaron became legendary *Hall of Fame* professional baseball players, they first went through the "process" of learning the fundamentals of the game called *baseball*. Before an Olympian wins a gold medal he or she first must go through a *process*. The process consists of uninterrupted practice, discipline, mental and physical toughness, and personal commitment to excellence. Success is a process. To succeed in anything, you will need to go through the process of learning what it takes to succeed.

GET READY. GET SET...START!

One of the most challenging elements of progress is *starting*. Though *starting* is an easy task, some view *starting* as being one of their most difficult tasks to conquer. There are people – young, old, married, divorced, single, women, and men – who know exactly what they want to achieve. Though they know what they want to achieve, when the time arrives for them to convert their wants into physical action, the *thought of starting* either derails or stops them from beginning the process.

Recently, I was introduced to a gentleman named Larry. While talking with Larry, he enthusiastically told me about how he had already mentally created his forthcoming success. In Larry's mind, he knew what he wanted to purchase once he reached a certain level of success. He knew the model and color car that he wanted to buy. Larry had visualized the exterior and interior design of his new luxury dream house, as well as his summer home. With everything *mentally* envisioned and aligned, it was time for Larry to take physical action toward the images he mentally sculpted in his mind. Then suddenly in the midst of our conversation, Larry instantly stopped talking. It was as though he had mentally placed his vision on pause. What happened?

It was the thought of taking physical action that made Larry slam on his mental brakes. Although Larry knew exactly what he wanted to achieve *mentally*. His challenge arrived when he realized it was time for him to *start taking physical action* toward what he had mentally envisioned. What happened to Larry is a universal scenario that takes place on a daily basis. There are millions of people who know exactly what they want to *mentally* achieve; however, they refuse to put forth the physical effort that will enable them to transform their *mental* wants into physical achievement.

Progress thinkers are self-motivated and action-oriented. They are eager to make things happen, as they take action toward their dreams and ideas daily. The physician, lecturer and author Oliver Wendell Holmes, Sr. once stated, "The mode in which the inevitable comes to pass is through effort." As a progress thinker, you will need to put forth the physical effort to succeed. If you don't put forth the physical effort toward what you want to achieve, your *wants* will become "won't" results. In other words, your progress and success *won't* happen until you start taking physical action toward what you *want* to happen. To succeed, you must *start* taking action. Thinking about what you want to achieve is one aspect of success. Taking action toward what you are *thinking* about will enable you to physically succeed.

START THE FORWARD PROCESS

Whatever you want to achieve, you first must start the *process* to achieve it. At the beginning stage, you don't have to take gigantic steps. You can simply start by taking small and productive steps.

A round ball will either roll forward, backward, or side-to-side. Which direction will you roll your ball? Push your ball *forward*. Every step you take will either place you closer or distance you from your achievements. Taking *forward steps* will place you closer to what you want to achieve. When you take forward steps, you will progressively move closer to achieve your goals. It doesn't matter the size of the steps you take–big or small. What matters the most is that you *start* taking the steps that will enable you to succeed in your life. Taking a single *step forward* will be more productive than not taking a single step at all.

Remember, you must *start* the process to make progress. When you think forward, your actions will begin to move you forward. To advance your progress, you must be willing to take the initial action forward. When you take one step forward toward your dreams, your dreams will take one step forward toward you. The action steps you take forward (not backwards) will place you closer to achieving what you desire.

4

THINK PROGRESS,
NOT LIFE TRAPS

*"If you don't have a positive outlook,
something negative will grab you."*
–MICHELLE SCOTT

In this chapter, we will talk about various *life traps*. Life traps are self-defeating behavior patterns, which deter countless people from taking action in their lives. You may have heard of a few of the life traps: Fear, complaining, denial, procrastination, blaming others, and negative thinking are just a few life traps that millions of people encounter in their lives on a daily basis.

Most people think life traps occur on the outside of them; however, the majority of life traps take place internally. Life traps can internally entrap you inside an invisible cage, if you allow them to control you. For example, although we cannot physically see fear, many of us become fearful. Think about it. If you had never heard, seen, or knew what the word "fear" meant would you still be fearful? *Fear is a reflection of what your mind believes.* If you mentally believe you are afraid, you will become afraid. If you believe you will succeed, you will succeed. As I've stated to audiences, "We were taught how to be *fearful*. Now, we need to teach ourselves how to become *fearless*."

Fear is something we learned and picked up from others. For example, while growing up, we observed our parents, friends, and television. We noticed how certain people said, "I'm *afraid* of scary movies" or "I'm *afraid* of heights." Although each person said the words, "I'm *afraid*" at different times the words and beliefs continue to appear within our minds.

When was the last time you took a personal survey and asked yourself, "What am I *afraid* of?" If you don't conquer your fear, your fear will conquer you. You are the captain that controls the on and off switch to your own fears and life traps.

BEYOND THE FEAR TRAPS

As William Faulkner, the novelist and poet once said, "We have to start teaching ourselves not to be afraid." For years, people have tried to tell us what to be *afraid* of in our lives. Some of us listened and became afraid, while some of us disregarded the attempt and became brave.

As kids growing up, some of us heard our parents or the people around us utter phrases such as, "I'm *afraid* of spiders" or "I'm *afraid* to fly on an airplane" or "I'm *afraid* of this or that." Today, as grown-ups, many of us continue to allow those same words, "I'm *afraid*" to linger in the midst of our minds.

You are the only person who controls your life, so what are you afraid of? Don't give fear the satisfaction of controlling you. Give yourself satisfaction by taking control of your fear. You have more control over your life than you think. Whatever you are afraid of you can overcome. You can remove your internal fear traps. Fear traps are not the dominant controller over you. *You* are the dominant controller over your fear. The only way fear will be able to control you is if you allow it to control you. When your mind is focused, your faith is strong, and your actions are moving toward what you want to achieve, what is there to fear?

BECOME FEARLESS

Denial, procrastination, blaming others, and negative thinking are all internal *life traps*. Not only are they "life traps," they are also *fear traps*. It's the *fear* within you that will continually trap you from enjoying your life. One reason people doubt themselves is because they *fear* themselves. Doubters usually don't trust others or themselves. They habitually doubt themselves, their potential, and their possible outcome.

The majority of the people who procrastinate often *fear* the thought of change. Procrastinators would rather delay or put off taking the actions that will change, improve, or advance their lives to a new level. Most people who blame others tend to *fear* the thought of taking full responsibility for their own actions and results. Instead of taking responsibility for their own actions and results, they find a way to blame someone else for their actions and results. Have you ever noticed whenever the end results are unrewarding or not pleasurable enough, how some people will blame someone else for their results? Using the phrase, "It's not my fault" is what I call the *blame mentality*. If you enjoy blaming others, when are you going to take the initiative and start blaming *yourself* for your own actions and results?

The people who think negative tend to fear a positive outcome. Negative thinkers always have a choice to think positive. Nevertheless, most negative thinkers choose to think in a negative manner. Negative thinkers aren't born with a *negative* mind. We are all born with *neutral* minds. Negative thinking and fear are both mentally learned, which means our minds can be taught and conditioned to think in a positive and fearless manner.

In her book *Feel The Fear and Do It Anyway*, Susan Jeffers wrote, "When you've finally mastered something and gotten rid of the fear, it will feel so good you will decide there is something else out there you want to accomplish." One effective way to succeed is to become fearless. Successful people overcome their internal fears by believing in themselves. In order to succeed, you must believe in yourself. When you believe in yourself, you will enhance your self-confidence to conquer your fears, which will enable you to become fearless. As a progress thinker, become fearless! The more you believe in yourself, the more you will go beyond your internal *fear* traps, procrastination, thinking negative, and blaming others.

COMPLAIN. COMPLAIN. COMPLAIN.

How many people do you know who *complain* all the time? Regardless of the situation–good or bad–they will always find something to *complain* about in their lives.

Have you ever noticed some people will *complain* and stress themselves out on a daily basis? Rather than doing something to change their lives, they would rather *complain* about their lives. For instance, people *complain* about their jobs. They *complain* about the traffic to and from work. They *complain* about their coffee being too hot or not hot enough. They *complain* about the weather. They *complain* about the day being too long (although every day has 24 hours in it.) They *complain* about everything, anything and everyone, but they refuse to *complain* about themselves.

I will admit that I've had my share of complaining, which I noticed got me nowhere, I have called companies to complain about their products and services, only to hear the person on the other end repeatedly say, "I understand." I have complained to my friends about certain things, only to hear them say, "I'm sorry to hear that." One lesson that I learned about complaining: complaining doesn't produce effective results. Complaining may give you some results, but it won't give you the best results. What are some of the things that you're *complaining* about? Ask yourself, "Are the things I'm complaining about really worth complaining about?" As the title of Richard Carlson's book states, *"Don't Sweat the Small Stuff."*

There are millions of people who are far worse off than we are, so why are we complaining about the small stuff in our lives? As Americans, we have endless privileges that countless people around the world dream about. Yet, many of us complain about the privileges that we do have in America. For example, there are people who live in third world countries that lack education, food, water, and electricity. In America, we can turn on and off our lights at any given moment by the flip of a switch. In America, we can take showers and/or baths–which ever one we choice to use on that day–with clean running water. In America, many of us are able to eat three meals, plus snacks, on a daily basis. In America, children are able to attend public or private schools to receive their education, and attend college after graduating from high school. In America, adults are able to go back to college, at any age, so they can continue their education. Think about it. How is it that many people who live in third world countries–who don't have more than us Americans–*do not complain* about what they *don't* have in their lives, while many of us Americans *complain* about what we *do* have in our lives?

One reason why some people complain, think negative, and doubt themselves is because they are not maximizing their full potential. When it comes to progress, many people will go through the *mental* motions to succeed, but they refuse to maximize their *physical* motions to succeed. Once you start maximizing your potential, you will begin to minimize and delete your complaining. Why? Because when you maximize your potential, you won't have anything to complain about.

Complaining is a choice, which you can choose to halt at any moment in your life. One effective way to stop complaining is to decide that you will stop complaining. The secret to making progress is not to *complain* about your life, but to *improve* your life.

As a progress thinker, start participating in tasks that will improve your life daily. When you strive to improve yourself every day, you will begin eliminating the complaining out of your life. The more you improvement yourself, the less you will have to complain about. Make today a complain-free day.

THE BLAME GAME

We have all seen and heard of "the blame game." *The blame game* is when a person places the blame on someone else. This usually occurs when someone experiences unwanted results such as defeat and/or embarrassment. The *blamer* will quickly blame others; however, he or she will refuse to blame oneself for the unwanted end results.

I like the way the author Erica Jong described the blame game: "Take your life in your own hands, and what happens? A terrible thing: no one to blame." Think about it. If you didn't have anyone around you to *blame*, whom would you seek to place the blame on for your unwanted results? Are you someone who takes full responsibility for your own actions and results, or do you seek ways to blame others for your personal actions and results? If you are constantly blaming other people for your *own* results, when are you going to remove yourself from behind your personal life traps? Stop blaming others. Start deleting the life traps.

Though the Statue of Liberty is located in New York City, it holds the torch of freedom for all throughout the world. As human beings, we must be willing and strong enough to stand up in the world, so we can begin to hold our own individual torch. We are the captains of our actions, results, and life. The same way every captain is in charge of the boat, *you* are the captain who holds the steering wheel to your own life, progress, and success. As the captain of your life, you are responsible for your own actions and results. If you're not producing the results you want in your life, the only person that you can blame is *yourself.* Instead of asking yourself, "Why me?" Start asking yourself, "Why not me?" Become the person who will acknowledge and accept accountability for your own decisions, actions, and results.

As a progress thinker, every action, result, and change pertaining to your life starts with *you*. If you are unhappy with your life, *you* can improve and alter it, and enjoy a better and happier life. Nobody can live your life for you. *You* are the only person who can determine your own destination. *You* are in charge of the direction and the destination in which you want your life to sail. As the captain of your life, put your boat in the water and take charge.

5

THE BIG THINKERS

*"I like thinking big. I always have. To me,
it's very simple. If you're going to be thinking anyway,
you might as well think big."*
–DONALD J. TRUMP

There are over six billion people throughout the world. Among the multitude of people in the world, it's usually the person who *thinks big* and *takes action* toward his or her big vision that standout from the large crowd.

There is a big difference between "thinking" about what you want to achieve, and "taking physical action" toward what you want to achieve. *Thinking* about what you want to achieve will mentally get you <u>to</u> the starting line. *Taking physical action* toward what you want to achieve will physically get you <u>across</u> the achievement line.

Big thinkers do big things. Big thinkers are people with big ideas and visions. Big thinkers usually think beyond the norm by designing their own pathways that will ultimately lead them to what they want to achieve in their lives. Most importantly, big thinkers take action toward their big vision, until they transform their mental vision into physical existence.

Thinking big and taking physical action are both necessities for achievement. Begin to think bigger. When you mentally and physically aim toward bigger achievements, you will eventually hit the big target called *success*.

TWO DIFFERENT THINKERS

What is the difference between a *big thinker* and a *small thinker*? Big thinkers refuse to place mental limits on their vision because they know limits will prevent them from producing extraordinary results. Small thinkers always place mental limits on their vision that is why small thinkers constantly produce small or no results.

The author Frances Moore Lappe defined small thinkers with the following words: "The only real risk is the risk of thinking too small." This reminds me of one afternoon during a business meeting, when two successful businessmen were casually talking about business and how they could collaborate to amplify their companies. In the midst of their conversation, one of the businessmen mentioned a mutual person, which they both knew. The businessman stated to the other, "George is a great person, but he *thinks too small* to fit the caliber that will help us grow."

> *"You can either think small or think big.*
> *The height of your thoughts will produce*
> *the height of your actions and results."*

As a progress thinker, will you think big or think small? The choice is yours. Become a *big thinker*, not a small thinker. The majority of all successful people are big thinkers. Michelangelo, the renowned artistic painter, sculptor, and architect, knew what thinking big meant when he said, "Lord, grant that I may always desire more than I can accomplish." When you go for more in your life, you will accomplish more on your journey.

As a progress thinker, you can either think small or think big. The height of your thoughts will produce the height of your actions and results. Don't be afraid to dream big. There is nothing wrong with having oversized dreams. Having big dreams indicates you are ready to grow in your life. Big dreams are like a pair of shoes one size too big–there is always room available for you to grow into them. Despite how many people tell you that your dreams are too big–keep dreaming big! Go for your big dreams, especially, if your dreams are going to help you grow into a better person.

THE BIG THINKERS

EVERY VISION IS DIFFERENT

As human beings, our vision comes in various shapes, sizes, and colors. Some visions are bigger and more vivid than others. Big thinkers, also known as "big dreamers," are people who have passionately unleashed their minds to think bigger.

Big thinkers give themselves the permission to dream big. They open their minds to roam freely without limits. For example, a big thinker is like a driver of a convertible car with the top down on a long never-ending highway. In other words, big thinkers are open-minded people who refrain from putting limits on top of their huge ideas and visions.

As individuals, we have our own vision of what we desire to achieve in our own lives. When your vision of what you want to achieve differs from others, don't let that deter you from taking action toward achieving your own vision. Regardless of what someone else's vision may be, keep your mind focused on achieving your vision. The altitude of your progress and success begins within your mind and actions. You can accomplish anything and everything you desire, once you place your thoughts and actions outside of your mental limits. Take action toward your own vision today.

BEYOND THE LIMITATIONS

Every *limitation* starts with a personal thought. How tall do you allow yourself to think? This question may appear abnormal or broad; however, it's an inquiry that will expand your mental and personal limitations.

A reflection of the previous question from a different angle: Are you a person who places a certain height or limit on your mind? Words like, "I would but..." or "They said I couldn't do it" are not only negative words–they are also "limiting" words.

Have you ever noticed how some people will blame others for their own personal results? They blame others by using the words "They said." First of all, who are *they*? Secondly, it doesn't matter if *he, she,* or *they* said something–at the beginning and at the end of the day–*you* are the sole proprietor for your own life, actions, results, progress, and success.

You don't have to delete the word "they" out of your vocabulary; however, it's essential that you learn how to manage the word "they" in your vocabulary. For instance, whomever you classify as "they" – *they* cannot live *your* life for you. We are all responsible for our own personal lives. Throughout all the people who have entered your life–parents, husband/wife, kids, brother/sister, friends, boss, and co-workers–*you* are the only person who can live your life.

As a progress thinker, you must become the person who will stand up and take full responsibility for living and enjoying your life daily. You can exceed the limitations, once you commence to allow yourself to think taller. Think bigger and aim higher every day.

THE SECRET OF HIGH ACHIEVERS

There is one secret that all high achievers have in common: They never settle for what they accomplished yesterday. Here is the high achievers motto: "Whatever you accomplished yesterday is past tense today."

High achievers know every day is a brand new day to improve what they have already accomplished. This is one reason why they are called "high achievers." High achievers constantly strive to set higher standards for themselves to achieve on a daily basis.

It's in the midst of the "thinking" phase that high achievers are separated from the low achievers. For example, low achievers *give up,* before they reach the end. High achievers *keep going* until the end, no matter what happens. Strive to become a high achiever. You will begin to make more progress, once you start focusing your mind, energy and actions on improving yourself daily.

Since every day is a brand new day, why not aim higher than you did yesterday? There is always something else that you can achieve. As I like to say, "There is always a *next* level." As a progress thinker, what is your next level? What will you achieve today that will exceed what you accomplished yesterday? Last week? Last year? The more you keep surpassing what you accomplished the day before, the faster you will join the ranks of the high achievers.

EXPECT THE BEST

Sam Walton, the founder of Walmart, hit the nail on top of the head when he said, "High expectations are the key to everything." There are numerous ways to make progress, but having high expectations for yourself should be placed at the top of your list.

When I start my day, I literally tell myself, "I *expect* to have an outstanding day no matter what happens." Why do I start each day with the previous phrase? Because expectancy creates its own rewards. Yes, I may encounter a few challenges within the day, but I don't let that interrupt or ruin my day. After telling myself, "I expect to have an outstanding day no matter what happens" that instantly becomes one of my daily goals.

In the Bible, Proverbs 24:14, states, "So shall the knowledge of wisdom be unto thy soul: when thou hast found it, then there shall be a reward, and thy expectation shall not be cut off." There is nothing unrealistic about expecting to achieve your dreams and goals. Progress thinkers reach success because they expect to succeed. Successful people always *expect* to succeed.

Self-expectancy is essential to making progress. Nothing can stop the people whose expectations are to succeed because their confidence, determination, and action will make them thrive. Begin to fuel your expectations with determination and confidence. The level of your confidence and determination to succeed will produce the level of your actions and achievements.

When you set high expectations for yourself, you will need to follow through with action toward your expectations. It will be your actions toward your expectations that will produce the results you expect. In order to have an outstanding day, you must expect to have an outstanding day. Start each day by announcing to yourself, "I *expect* to have an outstanding day no matter what happens!" Repeat it to yourself, while brushing your teeth, putting on your make-up, combing/brushing your hair, and while getting dressed.

When you *expect* to have an outstanding day, you will discover creative ways to make your day outstanding. Regardless of the roads you've traveled on in your life – good or bad – you will reach your destination, when you enhance your expectations.

DID YOU FILL IN THE BLANKS?

As human beings, all of us have our own thoughts about life. I believe *life is a gigantic fill in the blank test*. Although life is filled with many challenges, obstacles, and hardships—we must individually seek and discover our *own* answers to pass our *own* test in life daily.

Life constantly gives us our own *fill in the blank* tests. Every day life presents us with various challenges and obstacles that make us question ourselves. This is all a part of the test. During every test, *we must personally fill in our own answers to the blanks in our own lives*.

There is a lesson ready to be learned within life's daily challenges. For example, as students, we took various tests such as Math, Science, and History. Many of the tests that our teachers handed us were either multiple choice or fill in the blank. It was great, if you knew all of the answers. However, it wasn't so great, if you forgot to study for the test. Life doesn't give you the answers to your test, you have to seek and discover them on your own, which is part of the learning process.

One lesson I noticed about life: Life is a fill in the blank test, which requires you to study yourself. Yes, you will be challenged on your journey. When you take your daily fill in the blank test, avoid writing the words, "I give up," "I quit," or "I can't" as your answers. When your objective is to succeed, don't defeat yourself before you succeed. Whenever you say, "I give up," "I quit," and "I can't" you instantly defeat yourself because these are self-defeating words. In order to succeed, you must eliminate the negative thoughts that could defeat you.

The next time life hands you a test, and you don't know the answer, don't give up—keep your head up. Champions refuse to give up. You are an extraordinary person, which makes you an extraordinary champion. Always keep your mind focused on the goals you want to achieve. The secret to every success is to keep moving forward. When you keep moving forward, you will continually pass the tests that life place in front of you.

BELIEVE TO SUCCEED

One of the primary steps on every progress and success ladder is to *believe*. Progress thinkers are believers. They believe in themselves and what they want to achieve. As a progress thinker, you will need to believe in *who* you are, *what* you are, and *what you are aiming to achieve*. Your beliefs will take you to any destination that your mind and actions desire.

It's been said, "The mind is like a magnet and if your beliefs are strong enough, you will physically attract what you want into your life." Progress thinkers understand they must believe in themselves to succeed. If you took a personal survey on yourself, how would you answer the following question? Do you *believe* in yourself or do you *doubt* yourself? To succeed in anything, you must believe in yourself and what you want to achieve. Doubting yourself will derail you from succeeding. Believing in yourself will empower you to succeed.

You can turn anything into reality, when you believe in the reality. Nothing is impossible to the person who constantly believes in oneself. If believing in yourself is a challenge, ask yourself, "What is holding me back from *believing* in myself?" Asking yourself the previous question will enable you to discover your personal hurdles, so you can understand and overcome them. We succeed when we believe in ourselves. For example, a friend told me that she lost weight because she *believed* she could lose weight. In order to make effective progress you will need to wholeheartedly believe in yourself. One way to believe in yourself is by removing *doubt* from your mind. How do you remove doubt? By believing in yourself daily.

Believing in yourself is essential. As I recently stated to one of my friends, "Put on your *beliefs* and wear them with pride." How much pride do you have in your beliefs? Are you *strengthening* your beliefs daily or are you letting your beliefs *whither* daily? As a progress thinker, you will need to enhance your self-confidence, grow comfortable with your personal decisions, and believe in yourself, even when others don't believe in you. You can make your beliefs stronger than your doubts. The more you believe in yourself, the stronger you will build your self-confidence. It will be the quality of your own belief system that will build the bridges to your own success.

6

EXCUSES WILL CLOSE DOORS ON YOUR PROGRESS

"There are a thousand excuses for every failure,
but never a good reason."
–MARK TWAIN

In chapter 5, we talked about *the big thinkers*. There is an additional element you will need to know about the big thinkers: Big thinkers refuse to make *excuses,* because they do whatever it takes to avoid making excuses.

In this chapter, we are going to talk about excuses and how they can affect your performance and outcomes. Most of us have either heard or made an excuse once upon a time in our lives. When I was a kid, I made my share of excuses. As an adult, I've verbally and mentally eliminated making excuses, which means I no longer make excuses for my actions and results. Why? Because I noticed that excuses are nothing to be proud of and they will only get you so far, so why make them?

If you had never heard of, or seen the word "excuses" before, would you still make *excuses* in your life? Most people don't fail because of their "reasons." They fail because of their *excuses,* which they label as their *reasons.* The following question has been asked over and over again, "What separates successful and unsuccessful people?" Successful people refuse to make excuses for their actions and results. Unsuccessful people constantly make excuses for their actions and results. If you make excuses why you *can't* succeed, stop making excuses because you *can* succeed. When you know what you want to achieve, you must throw away your excuses to achieve it.

Progress thinkers make the most progress because they do whatever it takes to avoid making excuses. When you know deep within yourself that you have done your best–given your all–you won't have to make any excuses because your actions and results will speak for you. Strive to make progress, instead of excuses.

THE BOX OF EXCUSES

There are various ways to succeed, but making excuses is not one of them. Excuses are like useless toys sprawled all over the floor that should be picked up, placed inside of the *excuse box*, and kept inside the box. Babies usually leave their toys out because they don't know better. As adults, we are responsible for picking up our own toys. For some people, their "excuses" are their toys. For instance, the person who makes *excuses*, pulls his or her excuses out of the box, when he or she wants to play with them, and leaves them out for someone else to pick them up.

Excuses will stop a rabbit from hopping. Can you imagine a rabbit making an *excuse* for not hopping? It may sound silly. However, making excuses is silly too. Hopefully, you are beginning to see and understand how unnecessary excuses are when they are used to display and replace your actions.

DELETE THE EXCUSES

An *excuse* is the replica of a bad habit, meaning it's not good for you. Did you make any excuses today? If so, how many excuses did you make today? If you made one excuse today, you have made one excuse too many. It will be your excuses that will place a damper on your progress.

What usually happens when an excuse is made? When people make an excuse, they usually blame anyone and everyone, except themselves. Do you find yourself blaming others for your results? If so, when are you going to stop blaming others for your own personal results? Despite how many people you may attempt to blame for your personal results, you are always responsible for your own actions and excuses.

Making excuses is one of the major challenges in life. Many people think their challenges start on the outside of them. One thing you must know about excuses: Your excuses don't start on the *outside* of you. Your excuses start *inside of your mind* before exiting your mouth. How do you think you will succeed if your mind is constantly being occupied with excuses? Don't let excuses rent a room in your head.

> *"An excuse is like cow manure;*
> *it smells bad and nobody wants to be around it."*

You can sugarcoat many things, but you can't sugarcoat your excuses. An excuse is like cow manure; it smells bad and nobody wants to be around it. Excuses are sliding boards to failure. Excuses will keep you from reaching success. Excuses will make people close and lock their doors because they are tired of hearing your excuses. To make successful progress in anything, you must stop making excuses. Once you delete the excuses, more doors will begin to open for you.

If you make excuses, it's time to delete the excuses out of your life. Nothing successful gets accomplished whenever an excuse is present. When your desire is to succeed, remove all the excuses from your mind and vocabulary. Keep in mind that you can succeed, once you stop making excuses why you can't succeed. In other words, you can achieve your goals and dreams, once you throw away your excuses. To move forward, you must leave your excuses behind you.

Every progress needs effective results to succeed. When you want to turn your dreams and goals into reality, you will need to remove the excuses from your mind. Mentally subtracting your excuses will allow you to physically multiply your progress and success. To maximize your progress in business, finances, relationships, and life you must eliminate your excuses.

Once you delete your excuses, you will advance your progress. Write the words, "No More Excuses!" on a piece of paper and place it where you can see it daily. The next time you want to make an excuse for something, simply tell yourself, "No More Excuses!"

7

SCHOOL OF HARD KNOCKS

*"Regardless if you have encountered a hard
knock or a soft knock, it's still a knock.
How will you handle your knocks?"*
–SKIP J. WILLIAMS

Every road in your life won't be smooth or straight. There will be times when life will present you with curves, detours, under construction signs, rough terrain, and uncomfortable roads on your paths. When it comes to your journey, you will need to design and build your own roads to reach your destination.

On a daily basis, we are constantly faced with challenges. Many of us are faced with mental, financial, emotional, physical, spiritual, family and/or professional challenges. Some of us are faced with a combination of all the challenges at the same time. There are some challenges that we will understand, and there are some challenges that we will never understand. Sometimes we need to go through challenging moments to understand the logic behind the experience.

Les Brown, the motivational speaker and author, stated, "When life knocks you down, you should always try to land on your back–because if you can look up, you can get up!" Many of us have seen sporting events played in-person and/or on television. Some of us have participated in sports. As progress thinkers, we are playing in the stadium called "Life." Everything within the stadium is a metaphor of *life*. When we step up to the plate called *life*, we have a choice: We can either swing the bat or hold the bat. *Life* will either throw us a curve ball, a fastball, or a change up. Whatever *life* decides to throw at us, we must be ready for it.

Every challenge we encounter has its own way of making us take immediate action. For example, when you want to take your time to do something a life challenge will come along and make you speed up your pace. It doesn't matter which direction you go in life, there will always be challenges on your journey. Challenges occur in different sizes, shapes and scenarios. Despite the height, width, and amount of challenges that life places in front of you—you can prevail your personal and professional life challenges.

MY PERSONAL HARDSHIPS

The majority of us have experienced some form of hardship in our lives. A few of us call our *hardships*: adversity, bad luck, hard times, problems and potholes. This is an area that no one likes to talk about, and they will do just about anything to avoid talking about it. Everyone goes through some type of adversity, however, most people don't like to talk about his or her personal hardships. Adversity doesn't make you a bad person. In fact, adversity can help you grow into a better person.

I will admit that I've hit plenty of potholes in my own life, and I'm not talking about the potholes that your car tires run over in the street; I'm talking about adversities. You're probably thinking, "What does Skip Williams know about hard times?" Believe me, I know plenty about hard times. Like the saying goes, "You have to start somewhere." In my personal and professional life, I didn't start at the top of my own success mountain. I started at the bottom and worked my way to the top.

There was a time when I was at rock bottom, literally. Although I was down, I never counted myself out. Yes, I struggled along the way; nonetheless, I still found a way to overcome my adversities. I never gave up on my dreams or myself. For example, I've been evicted out of my own relative's household. I've been on the unemployment line more than a couple of times. I've filed bankruptcy. The woman I loved dearly and wanted to marry left me and married someone else. There were times in my life, when I had to count pennies just to buy food to eat <u>one</u> meal for the day. Though *water* is not eatable, there were times when I only had *water* for breakfast, lunch, and dinner. Nevertheless, I worked with what I had available to survive the hardships that I was going through.

When it comes to adversity, it doesn't just happen to you, the middle-class, or to the poor. Adversity happens to everyone, even to the wealthy people. Hardship extends beyond just *personal finances*. Hardships also relate to personal emotions, relationships, health, divorces, homelessness, lack of knowledge, and loss of jobs. As I previously mentioned, "Hardship is a part of life that most people don't want to talk about." The only difference between people with hardships is that some people *"will tell you"* when they are going through hardships, while others *"will refuse to* tell you" when they are going through hardships.

HOW HARDSHIPS WILL CHANGE YOUR LIFE

I recall working at a particular job, where my working hours were from four in the afternoon to midnight. One day upon arriving to work, I decided to up and quit my job with only $68 to my name. Did I view myself as a quitter? No. Why not? Because I had reached a point in my life where I felt it was time for me to venture out and try something new. Plus, I was tired of going to the same boring job just to receive a paycheck that was barely paying my bills.

In the midst of my hardships, I lived inside of a room at a boarding house for several years with a TV that didn't work for three years. I quickly learned that when you can't afford something, sometimes you have to do without, until you can afford it.

When I thought things couldn't get worse in my life it did. While I was living in New Jersey, my Grandfather passed away in my hometown (Decatur, GA). I was so financially broke that I had to borrow the money to purchase the airplane ticket to attend my own grandfather's funeral.

As I stood in front of my grandfather's casket with tears falling from my eyes, I made my grandfather a promise. I promised my grandfather that I would "take care of my grandmother." I didn't know how I was going to take care of my grandmother, because all I had was $40 in my pocket. I loved my grandfather, and I wasn't going to break my promise that I made to him. From that moment on, the only thoughts that went through my mind were, "Take care of Grandma. Take care of Grandma." With limited money, taking care of my grandmother instantly became my top priority and one of my ultimate goals.

While on the plane back to New Jersey, I started thinking of various ways that would give me the opportunity to enhance my income, so I could overcome my financial challenges. When I arrived back to New Jersey, I was determined to do whatever it took for me to take care of my grandmother. Instead of sleeping, I was up preparing myself to maximize each day. There were days when I stayed up for thirty-six hours straight without sleep. Not only was I determined and focused, but I also became *obsessed* to keep my promise that I had made to my grandfather.

Though it's been over a decade since my grandfather has passed away, I continue to push myself to fulfill my promise to take care of my grandmother. As the founder and CEO of Skip Williams Communications, my schedule gets tight at times, but I still make time for my grandmother. Several times a week, I reach out and call my grandmother to check up on her. When she needs someone to talk to, I am her designated listening ear, so she can express her personal thoughts and feelings freely without interruptions.

The moral of the story: When you know *what* you want to achieve, you must continuously push yourself to overcome the adversities in your life. If you noticed, I was financially challenged, but I brainstormed and took massive action until I found a monetary solution. Hardships will compel you to take action–if you're ready or not. When you encounter adversity in your life, don't give up or run away from it. Stand up and face your challenges. It will be your determination to overcome your adversities that will ignite your self-esteem and self-confidence to breakthrough your hardships.

STAY AFLOAT DURING HARDSHIPS

During my hardships, most of the people that I knew and had considered my friends departed out of my life. It seemed as though they left me hanging on an outside clothesline like a pair of soggy socks. At the time, I didn't know what to do, but I knew that I had to keep moving onward in my life.

There was a moment in my life when I faced a crossroad, and I didn't know which way to turn next in my life and career. What did I do? I didn't complain, nor did I get frustrated. Why? I knew that it was my personal hardships that empowered me to learn how to grow as a person. In other words, the adversities that I experienced in life taught me how to become a stronger and more creative person. My hardships ultimately woke me up and showed me the way, when no one–friends, family, or a mentor–was in the vicinity to physically direct me in my life. This was the moment when I became my own navigator to seek, explore and discover who I was as a person and what I wanted to achieve in my life.

My life ship has definitely been hit hard on numerous occasions from multiple angles, before I discovered how to advance my life to the next level. Although I've been through a multitude of adverse challenges, I can honestly say, "I survived them." If I survived *my* hardships, you can survive *your* hardships.

> *"The depth of your struggle determines the height of your success. What you've been through creates a passion for what you are preparing yourself for."*
> –ROBERT KELLY

The R&B recording artist, songwriter and producer Robert Kelly, also known as R. Kelly, once stated, "The depth of your struggle determines the height of your success. What you've been through creates a passion for what you are preparing yourself for." In life, when you go through hardships, you can either let your *ship sink* or *fix your ship* to keep it afloat. Attending the school of hard knocks will teach you how to fix your own ship to survive in life. Attending the school of hard knocks taught me how to grow into an innovative and zealous person.

I could have crumpled during the time of my adversity, however, I didn't. Why didn't I quit during the hard times? First of all, I'm not a quitter. Lastly, I didn't quit during my hard times because I knew deep down within that I had a lot more to give of myself. Knowing that I had more to give mentally, emotionally and physically drove me to go for more.

When my life hit rock bottom that was one of my defining moments when I decided to change my life. My life felt as though I had been minimizing my potential, my dreams, my actions, and myself for years. I wanted to achieve more, so I changed my life by challenging and maximizing myself daily. For example, I started taking more productive action steps. I started doing new things. Going to new places. Meeting new people. I set new goals and higher standards for myself to achieve. Every day I read more books and magazines that I felt would be useful resources for me to advance my personal and professional knowledge. Researching and modeling successful people like Anthony Robbins, Oprah Winfrey, Donald Trump, Robert Kiyosaki, and others enabled me to enhance my own mind, actions, and results to conquer my adversities.

People have asked me "Why do I work so hard?" The main three reasons that I work hard: First reason, I want to give my audience and clients the best resources that will elevate them to the next level. Second, I am constantly challenging myself to get better every day. Lastly, I've been financially broke before and it wasn't a good feeling, and I don't want to experience that again. This explains why I wake up early and stay up late, because I am always pushing and improving myself, so I can surpass what I have already accomplished.

Going through the school of hard knocks will teach you how to grow stronger mentally, emotionally, physically, financially, and spiritually. Moreover, it will teach you how to advance your progress and succeed like a champion. When adversity appears in your life, don't give up; give your best. As a progress thinker, you always have more inside of you to give. Don't minimize your life; *maximize* your life. You can successfully overcome your hardships, when you maximize your actions like a champion.

REPLACING SORROWFUL THOUGHTS

There is nothing rewarding about *sorrowful thinking*. Sorrowful thinking will place depressing pictures on the walls of your mind. Here is a motto you can place on your *mental* wall: "Life is to be learned, lived, and enjoyed; not wasted in a bucket of sorrow."

If you are a sorrowful thinker, when are you going to remove all those old, sad, and daunted photos of memories from the walls of your mind? When are you going to place brand new, vibrant pictures, and happy memories on the walls of your mind?

Have you ever thought or talked about someone that you haven't seen in a long time, then one day out of the blue, you see the person or they call you? Some people call this a *coincidence* or *luck*. It's not luck or a coincidence. The same effect occurs in our own lives. Whatever we think about, we attract it into our lives. For instance, when you think *positive* thoughts, you will attract *positive* results into your life. When you think *negative*, you will attract *negative* results into your life. You are what *you* think. Whatever you think about – joy or sorrow, pleasure or pain, wealth or poverty – you will attract it into your life.

Mental progress is made with successful *thoughts*. Physical progress is made with successful *results*. We succeed when we stop thinking about failing. To succeed in anything, you must think about success more than failure. You will begin to accelerate your progress toward success, when you condition your mind with successful, instead of sorrowful thoughts.

As a progress thinker, you can replace your sorrowful thinking by mentally and physically focusing your energy on achieving your goals and dreams. When you make your thoughts enjoyable, you will make your life more enjoyable. Start thinking more in an optimistic manner, and less in a pessimistic manner. When you think with a positive mental attitude, you will go beyond your sorrowful thoughts to become successful in your endeavors.

DID SOMEONE SAY CHALLENGE?

As I mentioned previously, my life hasn't always been smooth sailing. Before starting my own company, I used to work various 9-to-5 and part-time jobs. At one point I was working three jobs at the same time. For instance, I had a full-time 9-to-5 job, which I worked Monday through Friday. Once I left my 9 AM to 5 PM job, I would go to my second job that started at 7 PM to 3 AM, which I also worked Monday through Friday. Then, there was my third job, which I worked on Saturday and Sunday. There are 168 hours in a week, which I was working 96 hours per week. You may be asking, "Did I ever get tired?" Yes, my mind and body got tired. There were times when my mind and body got so exhausted that I didn't even know which day it was–all I knew was that I had to go to at least one of my jobs, because I was literally working seven days a week. Yes, my mind and body was tired, but I kept pushing myself daily.

Although I was working three and various jobs, the majority of the jobs never mentally or physically challenged me. With the lack of a challenge comes boredom. I felt like I was losing my creativity because I wasn't being challenged enough. Today, I mentally and physically challenge myself every single day. Every day I look forward to taking on new and more challenges in my life. The more I challenge myself, the more progress I make. The more progress I make, the more I succeed. Yes, some days are more challenging than others, which is okay by me, because I love a good challenge. Also, every challenge that I encounter points me toward new, pleasurable, and prosperous levels in my personal and professional life.

As individuals, we are constantly being challenged daily. Here are just a few challenges that we encounter, on a daily basis:

- Not sticking to the diet plan to lose weight.
- Not going to the gym to workout.

- Making excuses.
- Learning how to save and invest money effectively.
- Getting new clients.
- Building and improving relationships.
- Worrying about employment and doubting oneself.
- Lack of spending quality time with family and friends.

Challenges are daily events, which should be written down on a daily To-Do list. For example, when it comes to writing our daily To-Do list or *daily goals*, we quickly write down the tasks that we want to achieve for the day. However, we forget to write down how we will achieve our daily challenges.

Speaking of challenges, did you *challenge* yourself today? When was the last time you mentally and physically *challenged yourself* to do something new and exciting in your life? Make challenging yourself a daily event. Why wait for someone or something to challenge you, when there are endless ways that you can challenge yourself? The most effective way to succeed is to start challenging yourself daily.

Challenging yourself will do more than display a new starting point for you. It will continuously advance you to new levels, which will give you the opportunity to achieve more. Join a local fitness center and start *challenging* yourself to physically workout – exercise your body – for at least 30 minutes per day or three times a week. *Challenge* yourself to create an additional financial source of income that will give you the opportunity to multiply your wealth. *Challenge* yourself to eat healthy foods and drink plenty of water. *Challenge* yourself spiritually to spend quality time with your Higher power for guidance. *Challenge* yourself to enhance your communication, people, thinking and overall skills. *Challenge* yourself to become a better person.

As a progress thinker, start *challenging* yourself mentally and physically every day. Regardless if you're currently unemployed, a single parent, or making around $35,000 per year – you can think bigger and achieve more in your life. Start *challenging* yourself to become a millionaire. Start *challenging* yourself to go beyond what you achieved yesterday, last week, and ten years ago. When you challenge yourself daily, you will make progress daily. The more progress you make, the more you will succeed.

YOU CAN OVERCOME YOUR CHALLENGES

As Dr. Martin Luther King Jr. once said, "The ultimate measure of a man is not where he stands in moments of comfort and conveniences, but where he stands at times of challenge and controversy." There will always be a challenge or controversy around the corner waiting to present itself to you. When that moment occurs, you must be comfortable enough with yourself to stand up to the challenge and controversy.

Challenges and controversy will either strengthen or weaken you as a person. When challenges enter your life, how will you view them? Will you look at your challenges from a positive or negative point of view? Will you look at your challenges from a success or failure point of view? The way you view your challenges will be the way you will react to your challenges.

The *Special Olympics* is a worldwide organization that is renowned for providing sports training and athletic competition year-round for children and adults with intellectual disabilities. Although the *Special Olympics* athletes have a disability, they all continue to challenge themselves to win every day in life. As the *Special Olympics* motto states: "Let me win. But if I cannot win, let me be brave in the attempt."

Wherever you go, there will be at least one challenge in the vicinity. Every day we experience various forms of challenges either advertently or inadvertently. For example, some of us encounter mental and physical challenges via exercising and making decisions. While some face financial and career challenges. When you're faced with challenges, what actions will you take to breakthrough your challenges? Whatever challenges are placed in front of you, you can overcome them. There is always more than one way to overcome a challenge.

A strong mind starts with a positive mind. There are millionaires and billionaires who could lose all of their money, and eventually regain it all back. You may be asking, "How is that possible?" Millionaires and billionaires can recoup their wealth, simply by using the same techniques they learned and applied the first time around. Once they implement the same strategy, they will be able to accumulate their wealth once again. This is why it's essential to research successful people, because not only do they leave clues (how they succeeded), but they have designed the blueprint for you to succeed as well.

As a progress thinker, research successful people, products and services that have endured challenges and controversy, and then model them. Study the achievers inside and outside of your profession. Read autobiographies and magazines in your industry, and publications like *Success*, *Forbes*, and *Entrepreneur*. The key to researching is to seek, discover, and implement what works best for you. Once you find what successfully works, start applying it.

FROM BOREDOM TO CHALLENGING ONESELF

Research studies have shown the majority of the people who lack a *challenge* at work and in relationships, usually experience boredom. Boredom can cause depression. Boredom is an indication that you need to be challenged. If you're "bored," you may need to change your routine and start *challenging yourself* more.

The *NFL Hall of Fame* quarterback, Terry Bradshaw, once declared, "When you've got something to prove, there's nothing greater than a challenge." Most people usually become bored at their jobs, simply because the job doesn't challenge them mentally or physically. This was one of the main reasons that I decided to launch my own company. The 9-to-5 jobs seemed to always bore me, because they didn't challenge me enough to want to be there.

It's interesting how a regular 9-to-5 (eight hour) job *bored* me, however, when it comes to my own company, I can work up to twenty-hours per day and love every second of it without getting bored. The reason I don't get bored at Skip Williams Communications is because I am perpetually being challenged, on a daily basis. Challenging myself is one secret to my success. I'm always looking for a new challenge. Every day I mentally and physically push myself to surpass what I achieved the previous day, week, month, and year before.

As a progress thinker, set goals that will extend your mind to think bigger. You don't have to wait for someone else to challenge you. You can literally challenge yourself every single day. When was the last time you challenged yourself? Challenging yourself is an effective way to overcome boredom. If you get bored easily, change your daily routine. Do something new today. Get active. Start exercising and jogging, read a new book, listen to a new genre of music, surround yourself with a new group of friends who are smarter, younger, older and wealthier than you are. The more you challenge yourself, the further you will distance yourself from boredom.

IT'S JUST ANOTHER CHALLENGE

There are an abundance of opportunities and challenges around us. Some people view *challenges* as a bad thing. Successful people view *challenges* as a good thing, simply because they know each challenge will lead them to new opportunities.

Challenges and opportunities are the essence of life, because they will take you anywhere you desire. Keep in mind even "the best" strive to get better. They get better by challenging and improving themselves daily. When the legendary NBA Hall of Famer's Michael Jordan, Larry Bird and Earvin "Magic" Johnson played professional basketball, everyone viewed them as the best, including me. However, in their minds, they knew they could get better, so they constantly pushed themselves and their teammates to work harder. Every day Michael, Larry, and Magic challenged themselves and their teammates to improve their performance and results. Their hard work resulted in multiple NBA Championship wins.

At this moment, you may be experiencing a few challenges in your life. You may be going through a few trials and tribulations. You may have tried something in your life and it didn't turn out exactly the way you planned. If your outcome wasn't successful the first time around that's not a reason for you to give up. There is never a reason to *give up* in life. For example, there are people who have suffered heart attacks, strokes, cancer, been homeless, and used to be addicted to drugs and alcohol. Though they went through hardships in their lives, many of them survived and overcame their adversity because they refused to give up. If you give up every time you encounter a challenge, you will miss the best opportunities in life.

Since we are talking about hardships, challenges, and *not giving up*, Liz Murray is an inspirational example to talk about. When Liz was growing up, she experienced calamity in her life. Her parents were drug addicts, and her mother died when she was a teenager. As a teenager, Liz became homeless, had little education and lived on the streets. Though her life was unbalanced like a seesaw, due to the numerous challenges that weighing her down, Liz found a way to survive.

Instead of giving up or becoming a drug addict, Liz Murray ignited her focus and determination to create a better future for herself. After her mother died, she decided to go back to school, and she worked extremely hard to receive her diploma. What makes Liz Murray's story so amazing is that through all of her adversities, she never gave up. With her refusal to quit attitude, she won a scholarship to Harvard University. Her life story was so inspiring that it was made into a movie called *Homeless to Harvard*.

A marathoner Kevin O'Rourke once stated, "Dream big, but allow yourself the opportunity to start small, and have your share of struggles in the beginning." Every successful person didn't achieve his or her dreams on the first day, nor was Rome built in a day. Progress thinkers understand success is achieved in increments, and not all at once. Dream big and keep aiming toward your dreams until you achieve them. Remember, every path in life won't be smooth and straight, so get ready for the forthcoming bumps, curves, detours, and under construction signs ahead. Challenges will present itself to you if you're ready or not. It's up to you to decide if you're going to give up or press on. The latter will enable you to prevail. All challenges have a learning experience attached to them. We learn, live, and grow through the challenges that we encounter in our lives. It's the progress thinkers who seek and discover ways to overcome their challenges. As a progress thinker, keep pressing onward.

8

THE TURNING POINT

"Everyone encounters a few stumbling blocks on his or her journey toward the top. The most successful people utilize the stumbling blocks as their stepping-stones to make it to the top."
–MOTHER HICKS

On every journey there are stumbling blocks. Some people view and classify stumbling blocks as a *bad* thing. Stumbling blocks are "building blocks" and "eye openers" that will show you how to elevate to the next level. Without stumbling blocks would you still take the necessary steps to succeed? We never know how high, low, or how many stumbling blocks will be on our paths. Some of us will encounter more than others. Regardless of the height or amount of stumbling blocks that may appear on your path, you can overcome them.

Success rewards those who overcome their stumbling blocks. Stumbling blocks are strategically placed into our lives to silently guide our present decisions and forthcoming actions. They are placed in our lives to see how we will handle them. How do you see yourself handling your stumbling blocks? Do you see yourself falling down or standing up to your stumbling blocks? It will be the stumbling blocks that will make or break you. They will either strengthen or weaken your faith. Stumbling blocks aren't placed into your life to make you fail. They are placed in your life to make you stronger, so you can succeed.

Don't let stumbling blocks keep you from succeeding in your life. To succeed, you will need to go beyond the obstacles in front of you. You will begin to rise above the obstacles once you start using the stumbling blocks as your stepping-stones to elevate to the top.

WHERE IS THE TURNING POINT?

Have you ever experienced a painful moment in your life when you said, "Enough is enough?" If so, you have definitely reached your *turning point*. Your turning point is your new starting point.

What is a turning point? A turning point is when you encounter a painful experience in your life that makes you say, "Enough is enough." A turning point is equivalent to an emotional wake up call. It's an emotional reaction that will instantly make you do whatever it takes to physically change the painful situation that you're currently going through.

One thing you need to know about a turning point: Every turning point will be different. As progress thinkers, we encounter our own individual turning points. For instance, your turning point will be different from my turning point, and vice versa. A turning point usually occurs when something painful and/or dramatic happens in your life that makes you emotionally say, "No more! Enough is enough."

When most people reach their turning point they use the phrases, "Enough is enough" or "I've reached my last straw" or "I can't take it anymore, I must change my life." My turning point arrived, when I got tired of going to the same boring, dead-end, energy draining, non-challenging, and low-paying 9-to-5 job every day. The paycheck that I was receiving barely paid my rent, literally. The day arrived when I told myself, "Enough is enough. From this moment on, I will do whatever it takes to change my life, so I can live and enjoy a better life."

Every *turning point* produces a new *starting point*. It's usually the turning point that empowers most people to start turning their downward failures into upward success. For instance, a friend named Kathy once told me how she reached her turning point in her life. She said, "Skip, I got tired of my husband getting drunk and physically abusing me in front of my kids, so I left him and filed for a divorce." As Kathy continued, she said, "Though it's been years since my divorce. I have remarried. My new husband doesn't drink, nor does he abuse me. I can honestly say that I am much happier in my life." If you notice from Kathy's scenario, she turned her negative into a positive.

All of us have our own individual turning points. You will know when you've reached your turning point, because it will mentally, emotionally and physically drive you to get off your laurels to start doing whatever it takes to change your life. Don't be afraid to turn your life around. That's the beauty of having a turning point–you can begin to enjoy your life. Your *turning* point will place you on a new path that will lead you to a new *starting* point to succeed.

MASTER YOUR BUTTONS

When you want to elevate yourself to the next level, you must become the *master controller* of your own life. As the master controller, you control all the buttons that will take your life to each and every level you desire.

We define our own success. What you call success may differ from what others define as success. For example, three people may enter an elevator on the same floor – the ground floor – at the same time. However, all three people on the elevator may not be going to the *exact* same floor. Each person will exit the elevator on different floors. The first person may exit the elevator on the 2nd floor. The next person may exit on the 5th floor. The last person may exit on the penthouse level. In order to reach one's own individual destination, every person must decide when to get on and off the elevator. Only then will they find themselves on their desired floor of success.

There will be a few people who will attempt to press your *internal* buttons by emotionally getting on your nerves. This is one reason why it's essential that you control your master buttons. As the master controller, will you press your buttons to the penthouse level of pleasure and success? Or, will you remain on the ground level and allow others to press your pain and stress buttons? The choice is yours. As a progress thinker, you are more than the *controller* of your own life. You are the ultimate decision-maker to life's levels and destinations. Dream bigger and aim higher. Start putting elevators in your dreams. Press the buttons that will continue to hoist you to the next level in your personal and professional life.

ELIMINATE YOUR SANDBAG TO PROSPERITY

Surrounding yourself with the same people, on a daily basis, will give you the same results every day. This could be a plus or a minus in your life; it all depends on if you're encircling yourself with people who are helping you succeed or hurting your success. When your objective is to succeed, surround yourself with the achievers who will bring out the best in you.

Let's take a quick survey. The word "prosper" will be our focal point. Out of all the people that you associate with, how many people are helping you *prosper*? How many people are pulling you away from *prospering*? If you aren't prospering and receiving quality results every day, it may be time for you to upgrade the people that you're surrounding yourself with, on a daily basis. This might sound harsh. But, there are times when you will need to take specific actions and necessary risks to prosper.

Hypothetically, let's say that you were in the desert with limited food and water. Would you carry a multitude of heavy and unnecessary sandbags filled with *sand* in the desert with you? Of course not, why? First of all, there would be plenty of sand all around you. Lastly, the sandbags would slow you down. How many people are slowing you down from succeeding in life?

In business, no company wants to have excess overhead. In life, no person wants to have unnecessary and excess luggage. When you want to succeed in your life, you will need to drop the unnecessary and negative people out of your life.

> *"Get rid of anything less than excellent in your life,*
> *and your integrity will increase."*
> –BRIAN KOSLOW

As Brian Koslow once stated, "Get rid of anything less than excellent in your life, and your integrity will increase." Be honest with yourself; are you encircling yourself with the right people? If the people around are not helping you succeed, it may be time to drop your sandbags. Once you take the initiative and eliminate unnecessary people, places and things, you will start accelerating your progress, achievements, and prosperity.

SMART AFFILIATIONS

Affiliating yourself with resourceful people is one of the fastest ways to accelerate your progress to succeed. Many people call this concept "networking." It's also looked upon as creating your own success circle.

All of us know at least one person who is a little wiser and smarter than us, and who has accomplished one or a few things more than we have. One vital lesson I've learned: Just because someone has a little more wisdom than you that doesn't necessarily make him or her smarter than you. For instance, your friend might be more knowledgeable in one subject, while you're more educated in another subject. A good example would be the TV game show called *Jeopardy*. We usually see one contestant who will choose a category, and answer the majority of the questions in that one specific category. Why? Because the person was more knowledgeable in that one particular subject. Just because the person knew all the answers in one category doesn't necessarily mean that he or she is the smartest or will win the game.

You shouldn't get intimidated or become frustrated because someone may know a little more than you. If someone has more knowledge than you on a particular subject don't get upset or run from the person. Take the time to "learn" from the person.

We all have our unique *creative intelligence*. The secret to knowledge is to constantly look for ways to elevate your personal creative intelligence. If people are more experienced than you, allow them to help you succeed. Your "weak points" could be their "strong points." For instance, when you learn how to use other people's *strong points*, in return they will strengthen your *weak points*. There is nothing wrong with letting people help you, especially if their help will add strength, balance, and value to the weak areas in your life.

In his book called *Rich Dad, Poor Dad,* Robert Kiyosaki talks about how he learned to earn and invest money from his rich dad. Robert Kiyosaki succeeded because he placed himself around the right person (Rich Dad) and the right people (Advisors). They gave Robert valuable resources that enabled him to strengthen his weak areas. Robert Kiyosaki became wealthy by learning, applying, and enhancing his personal creative intelligence.

Seek and you shall find. Knowledge always finds the person who seeks it. Whatever you are looking for, it's looking for you. The more you seek innovative and valuable resources, the more you will discover the knowledge that will help you advance in your career, relationships, and triumphs. Surround yourself with creative and strong-minded people. They will give you an abundance of knowledge that will show you how to successfully advance your progress.

When you affiliate yourself with the elite, not only will you learn from the best, but you will also learn how to become one of the best. As a progress thinker, always seek the resources that will enhance your mind, productivity, and finances. When you receive new and valuable resources mentally and physically find a way to apply it. Once you begin to implement what you've learned, you will accelerate your progress to the fast lane, which will enable you to succeed faster.

DIVERSIFY YOUR FRIENDS

As kids, most of us heard the saying, "An apple a day will keep the doctor away." As adults, what are we doing to keep the "negative thinkers" away? One way to delete the negative thinkers out of your life is by encircling yourself with positive thinkers. Positive thinkers are exceptional gifts to have around you at all times. Keep in mind that you can never have too many positive thinking friends in your life.

My life changed when I learned how to diversify my life. To some people, the word *diversify* has a limited meaning. For instance, there are people who look at the word *diversify* only to describe their stocks, bonds, and mutual funds. The word *diversify* extends way beyond the stock market. When it comes to *diversifying,* it also pertains to how you think, and the people you associate with.

There is nothing wrong with adding *diversity* to your life. Opportunities present themselves when diversity is present. Diversity will add balance into your life. I learned how to balance my life by *diversifying* my life. For example, instead of reading books on one subject, I *diversify* my books by reading various subjects. Rather than listening to one genre of music, I *diversify* my music selection by listening to a variety of music.

Having the right people around you at all times is one of the best gifts that you could ever give yourself. Diversifying your friends is one of the most profitable investments that you will ever make. When you affiliate yourself with right people, you will begin to notice friends are assets. For example, I have friends who range from various sizes, shapes, races, and backgrounds. I have friends who are serious when it comes to business. I have friends who are comedians just by their natural character. I have friends who own their own companies, and friends who work for other companies. I have friends who are old, young, married, divorced, and single. Why am I telling you this? Because "diversity" doesn't have just one color, race, level, or definition attached to it.

Limiting your wisdom and friends will limit your progress, success, and wealth. You will advance your progress and success, once you start diversifying your thinking, friends, business, relationships and environments.

THE VALUE OF FRIENDS

When people ask me how can they succeed, I tell them, "Look for *valuable* friends." You can never have enough intelligent, optimistic thinking, and supportive friends in your life.

One reason most people don't succeed is because they associate with the wrong people. Surrounding yourself with the *wrong* people will take you down the wrong path. Surrounding yourself with the *right* people will place you on the right path.

"Friends are like software; both are upgradeable."

Creative, trustworthy, and supportive friends are valuable assets. It's good to have friends, but keep in mind friends are like software; both are upgradeable. Don't be afraid to upgrade the people around you. There is nothing wrong with upgrading yourself and the people around you. This is one of the secrets to success. Successful people constantly upgrade the people around them. When you *upgrade* your friends, you will *upgrade* your mind, actions, and results.

As a progress thinker, remove yourself from the negative thinkers who want you to fail. Develop your own success circle. Build relationships with people who want you to succeed. You will accelerate your progress once you encircle yourself with successful people and positive thinkers. Always look for golden opportunities to place yourself around successful people or in the vicinity of the achievers, because these will be the people who *can* and *will* help you succeed.

Successful people will share their wisdom with you, simply because they want to see you succeed. You may want to add a mentor to your success circle, because he or she will provide you with exceptional insight and strategies that will help you advance your progress, rewards and success to new levels.

9

WHAT ARE YOU WAITING ON?

*"Everything comes too late
for those who only wait."*
–ELBERT HUBBARD

There are various opportunities surrounding us at every moment. Some of us will see them, while a few of us will overlook them. Opportunities aren't lost because they are "not" present. Opportunities are lost because we "wait" for them to be present. Rather than *waiting* on opportunities to come you, sometimes you will need to create your own opportunities around you.

Every morning a mother drove her daughter to the bus stop and sat with her, until the school bus arrived. Then the girl would exit the car and ride the bus to school. On one particular morning the routine was shaken slightly. As usual, the school bus arrived on time. The mother leaned over to her daughter and gave her a hug and a kiss. After the hugs and kisses, instead of exiting the car, the little girl continued to sit in the front seat of the car, and simply looked out the window toward the bus.

The door of the school bus opened. All the other kids at the bus stop entered the bus. The door of the bus closed, then it departed. As the bus moved farther away from the bus stop, the mother sat looking at her daughter–in a dumbfounded manner–and said, "Sweetheart, is everything okay?" Turning toward her mother, the little girl replied, "Mom, everything is okay." The mother then said, "Sweetheart, the school bus just left. What are you *waiting* on?" The little girl stated, "Mom, when I'm with you I feel comfortable."

The moral of the previous story: There are countless people who are fully prepared to step outside of their comfort zone, however, they continue to sit inside of their comfort zone just like the little girl and

57

wait. Every person waiting at the bus stop will get on the bus, at least once, in his or her life. What are you doing with your life? Are you *waiting* for something to happen, or are you physically going out and making things happen in your life? If you're *waiting*, "What are you *waiting* on?" The longer you *wait* for whatever you are *waiting* on, the longer you will delay your arrival time to your destination called *success*.

THE DISADVANTAGES OF WAITING

Waiting for someone or something to come along and enter our lives is like waiting for an empty bucket to fill itself up with water. In other words, nothing happens until we take action to make it happen.

Let's place a magnifying glass on the word *waiting*. *Waiting* is exactly what it says, "WAITING." Think about it. Nothing occurs or gets accomplished during the "*waiting*" stage. *Waiting* is a form of procrastination. *Waiting* is an excuse. *Waiting* will hinder your forward progress into slow or no progress. *Waiting* doesn't put money in your pocket. *Waiting* will keep you in debt. *Waiting* will keep you from achieving your dreams, due to lack of action. *Waiting* will keep you standing in the same location, while everyone else moves forward.

What is the purpose of waiting? Waiting doesn't have a purpose. When you wait, not only will you miss all the fun, but you will also keep yourself from advancing and achieving more. The more you wait, the more you will procrastinate. The lesser you procrastinate, the more you will accomplish. In other words, you will accomplish more once you stop waiting.

> *"The lesser you procrastinate, the more you will accomplish."*

One of the best ways to overcome waiting is to become action-oriented. Over and over, I hear people say, "I'm too busy or I don't have time to workout." But, the same people find time to watch television. My schedule is tight, but I find time to workout, even if I don't make it to the gym. For instance, the next time you're watching TV, instead of sitting on the couch eating during commercial breaks, sit on the floor and do some crunches or sit-ups. Each commercial is between 30-60 seconds, so strive to push your mind and body for at least 30-60 seconds, which will be the equivalent of one commercial.

As a progress thinker, get in the habit of doing at least one set of sit-ups or crunches during the commercial breaks. Using this simple and effective strategy will do more than help you feel good; it will help you look good too.

WAITING TO MOVE OUT

In my profession, I have met adults between the ages of 21 through 60, who never left their parents' home. Since birth, they continue to live in the same household with their parents. Why are they still living at home with their parents? Could it be because they are going through some hard times? Maybe.

Every day I meet people who encounter hard times in their lives. Though the majority of the people are going through difficulties in their lives, many of them *refuse to* live at home with their parents. One reason some adults continue to live at home with their parents is because they are just "waiting" in life. They don't know what, why, or whom they're *waiting* for. Nevertheless, they continue to *wait* and live at home with their parents. Living at home with their parents has grown into a habitual comfort zone.

I remember talking with two adults–a brother and sister–who lived at home with their parents. While talking with them, I stated, "It's one thing to live at home with your parents when you're young or if your parents are ill. However, your parents are healthy and you're both grown adults." I continued by stating, "As adults, don't you think it's time for both of you to leave your parents' house?" Without saying a word, the brother and sister looked at each other. Then, I concluded with the following words, "Leaving your parents' house will show your parents, and yourself, that you can succeed on your own without their help."

A few weeks later, the sister took a big step in her life. She decided to move into her own apartment. The brother–the oldest of the two–continues to live at home with his parents.

Nothing gets accomplished when you *wait* on people, places, and things to come to you. There will be times when you will have to take the initiative and physically step outside your comfort zone to succeed. Progress starts once you decide to stretch (extend) your comfort zone. If you're comfortable *inside* of your comfort zone, you will be amazed with what's *outside* of your comfort zone. Don't be afraid to try something new. This is one reason why most people choose to reside in their comfort zone, because they are afraid to attempt something new. Extend yourself mentally and physically to learn and achieve new things.

Simply taking one step *outside* of your comfort zone will double your progress. Taking one step will be more productive than not taking a step at all. Stretching your comfort zone will make a big difference in your progress, because it will present you with new opportunities that will lead you to success.

MAKE IT HAPPEN

Progress thinkers are always seeking new opportunities to create and enhance their success. As a progress thinker, keep in mind that success doesn't start on the sideline. Success starts when you get on the field and make it happen.

Mary Kay Ash, the founder of Mary Kay cosmetics, once said, "There are three types of people in this world: those who make things happen, those who watch things happen and those who wonder what happened. We all have a choice. You can decide which type of person you want to be. I have always chosen to be in the first group." When you *watch* things happen, you automatically place yourself on the outside looking in. When you *wonder* what happened, you would have missed everything. When you *make things happen*, you will be in the midst of all the excitement. As the decision maker of your own life, which group will you choose?

As individuals, we are fully in charge and responsible for making our individual decisions. When your goal is to succeed you must create your success with your own mind. You can transform your dreams into reality, once you decide to make it happen.

While others are daydreaming about what they would like to achieve, take the initiative and make your dreams happen. Don't be a spectator by watching and wondering what happened. Today is your day to step up and start making things happen. If you want to become a leader or an entrepreneur, then make it happen. If you want to make more money, make it happen. If you want to buy a new car or home, make it happen. You can become a better parent or friend; make it happen. You can fulfill your dreams–make it happen. As a progress thinker, you can achieve anything that you desire, once you take the initiative and make it happen.

"GO" ACROSS THE ACHIEVEMENT LINE

How many people do you know who actually enjoy coming in "last" place? No one likes to come in *last* place, not even a horse. For example, a horse lost the horse race not because it was a slow or lazy horse. The horse lost the race because it was *waiting on* its jockey to tell it when to "GO!"

Think of your ideas, dreams, and goals as your *horse*. You are the jockey sitting on top of them. Your personal gate has opened for you to start moving toward what you desire. What will you do? Will you tell your horse to GO? Or, will you *wait* and remain at the starting line? If you have been *waiting* in your life, it's time for you to tell your horse to "GO!" Your progress and success are all waiting on you to tell them to "GO!"

To achieve anything, you must move toward what you want to achieve. NO ACTION = NO RESULTS! Every progress and success is accumulated through a form of action. It will be your actions that will produce your progress and success. Set your goals and take action toward your goals. Remember, you have places to go, people to see, and goals to achieve. Mount your saddle. Tell your horse to "GO!" Ride your ideas, dreams and goals across the achievement line.

WASTING TIME IS NOT AN OPTION

If you were to ask a high achiever how much time he or she wastes, on a daily basis, they would quickly tell you, "Wasting time is not an option for me." Successful people refuse to waste their time on unnecessary things. Do you think Bill Gates, Oprah Winfrey, and Donald Trump take on tasks that will waste their time? The answer...NO!

Successful people know how to optimize their mind, time, and energy productively without wasting their time. Instead of wasting time, high achievers will find productive tasks that will keep their minds and time from being wasted. For example, while sitting at the airport waiting to board an airplane, high achievers read books, magazines, newspapers, check and return e-mails, call family members and clients, as well as network with others.

Of course, there is a little sprinkle of "waiting" inside all of us. For instance, many of us *wait* while standing in line at the supermarket. We *wait* in traffic. We *wait* for our food to be cooked and served at our favorite restaurant. Some parents *wait* to pick-up their children from school and/or practice. Yes, there will be moments when "waiting" is required, but that doesn't mean we have to waste our time in the process. Instead of *wasting* your time, find something that's *worth* your time. You will make more progress once you begin to use your time more productively.

TODAY vs. TOMORROW

Benjamin Franklin, the author, scientist and inventor, once declared, "Don't put off until tomorrow what you can do today." Does the following phrase sound familiar to you, "Oh, I'll do it tomorrow?" How many times have you told yourself, "Oh, I'll do it tomorrow?" Once tomorrow arrived, you quickly said, "Oh, I'll do it tomorrow." Two days past, and you continue to sing the same old song, "Oh, I'll do it tomorrow."

We all know there are 24 hours in a day. *Waiting* to do something tomorrow is like placing your life and results on hold for a whole 24 hours. Why would you want to *wait* to live and enjoy your life 24 hours from now, when you can live and enjoy your life *today*?

There are numerous productive tasks that you can accomplish today *before* tomorrow arrives. Tomorrow's progress and results start with today's progress and results. Rather than *wasting* today, place your focal point on what will you achieve today. What will you achieve today? Will you...

- Learn a new language
- Network to meet new, valuable, and trustworthy friends
- Feed your mind with positive food
- Spend quality time with your family, friends, and pets
- Write your business plan to start your own company
- Call your local college to continue your education
- Start the diet you've always thought about

- Challenge yourself to overcome your internal fears
- Join the fitness center to exercise your body
- Create an additional income to build your wealth
- Produce new results to improve your life

Mentally and physically concentrate on the tasks that you will accomplish today. Tune out the unnecessary distractions. Forget about the negative things that happened yesterday. *Yesterday* is gone forever. Stop living in the past. Focus on today. Place your mental and physical attention on what you *will* and *must* accomplish TODAY!

FORWARD YOUR WAITING

Have you ever called someone – a client or the dentist office to make an appointment – and they either placed you on hold, or told you that they would call you back? If so, what did you do about it?

When I first launched my company, it was challenging because I didn't know anyone in my field, nor did I have any clients. There were times when I used to cold call prospective clients and they would say, "Mr. Williams, thank you for calling, but we will have someone call you back." When this happened, I made more phone calls. The more calls I made, the more I continued to receive the same song and dance, which entailed people not returning my phone calls. What did I do? I didn't get annoyed, nor did I stress myself out. I simply became more creative. Instead of waiting for clients to call me, I told myself, "Progress must be made." So, I called my local phone company and added the *call-forwarding* feature to my telephone.

The *call-forwarding* feature enabled me to use my time more productively. Rather than sitting around waiting for my office phone to ring, I started *forwarding* all of my phone calls to my cellular phone, which allowed me to get out of the office to conduct business face-to-face, and still receive my phone calls from my clients.

Don't wait for your success to come and ring your doorbell, because you will be waiting a long time. Whether in business or personal life, you must perpetually push yourself *forward* mentally, emotionally, and physically until you achieve what you want. When you want to achieve your goals, dreams, ideas, or meet new people–you will need to take the action steps that will lead you in that direction.

As a progress thinker, keep in mind that bigger opportunities will present themselves to you once you present yourself to them. To succeed, you must not *wait for* success, you must *move toward* success. Once you take the first step to achieve your goals, you will instantly begin the *forward* momentum to achieve them.

EVERY DAY IS A MYSTERY

Every day life presents its own mystery and rewards. We never know exactly what will happen today or what will happen tomorrow. The only thing we do know is what happened yesterday, and what we would like to happen today and tomorrow.

Every success story has an experimental background attached to it. For example, it took Steven Spielberg more than a few movies to become a legendary film director. Thomas Edison successfully created the light bulb. However, he didn't create it overnight or on his first attempt. It took Mr. Edison sleepless hours and over a thousand attempts to create the light bulb. Though Thomas Edison created the light bulb many years ago, today technology has enhanced the way that we use lights. Today, we use lights for everything via flashlights, headlights and brake lights in cars, ceiling lights, and lamps just to name a few things.

Every experiment creates its own legend. Each day is an experiment and we are the scientists. As the scientist of your life, what will you discover today? Will you discover your self-worth? Will you discover a new realm that will give you the opportunity to meet new people? Will you discover a new way to spend quality time with the people you care about? Will you discover how to volunteer your time to help others? Will you discover your personal strengths today? Will you discover how to enhance your communication and people skills? Will you discover how to increase your finances?

Every day may start off as a *mystery*; however, it doesn't have to remain a mystery. Each discovery that you make will display it's own unique value and rewards. Here is the secret formula for every success: *Keep Experimenting Until You Get It Right.*

10

GIVE YOURSELF PERMISSION

*"When we do the best that we can, we never
know what miracle is wrought in our life,
or in the life of another."*
–HELEN KELLER

Would you like to know the best-kept secret to how successful people increase their wealth? Build their self-confidence? Create endless relationships? Live their dreams? Reach happiness? Here is the best-kept secret to every success: GIVE YOURSELF PERMISSION!

High achievers always give themselves the permission to succeed. Giving oneself the permission to thrive is the starting line to every success. The importance of giving oneself the permission to succeed will be our focal point in this life-changing chapter.

In each one of us there is an extraordinary gift inside that is ready to be unwrapped, opened, and displayed for others to see it. As a progress thinker, you have a special *gift* within you. Every moment in your life you have the opportunity to show others, as well as yourself exactly who you are and what you represent as a person. Always remember, you are an authentic and special person, which makes you an overall unique person.

OPEN YOUR GIFTS

Many people don't succeed because they refuse to open their *internal gifts*. Don't be afraid to open your inner gifts. Give yourself the permission to unwrap and open the gifts within you.

Your personal success starts the moment you give yourself the permission to say, "I want to achieve more." As children, we waited for our parents to give us permission to go outside and to partake in activities. As adults, we need to start giving ourselves the permission to partake in new and adventurous activities. When you give yourself permission, you instantly give yourself the "authority" to mentally, emotionally, and physically prevail. When you give yourself *permission*, you give yourself the *authority* to excel forward on your journey. Once you give yourself the *authority*, your success will be endless because you will begin to discover new opportunities to achieve more. Plus, you will accelerate your progress to succeed faster in your endeavors.

As a progress thinker, you can achieve anything once you give yourself the permission to achieve it. Remember, giving yourself permission to succeed is equivalent to giving yourself the *authority* to succeed. When was the last time you gave yourself the "authority" to succeed in your own life?

You have an abundance of unique qualities. The key is to learn what your unique qualities are and then apply them. Don't waste your qualities. Start using your unique qualities. Give yourself the permission to open your personal gifts and discover your strengths, so you can commence to display your uniqueness today. Give yourself the authority to create a better life for yourself and your family. Unleash your personal authority. If millions of people have already given themselves the authority to achieve their dreams and goals, you can do it too.

YOUR BEST STARTS WITH YOU

It doesn't matter how many times you add, multiply, divide, or subtract the word "self" it will allows equal *self*. To make progress, you must give your*self* the permission to make progress.

Your success starts with *you*. Everything you want to achieve in life starts with *you*. If *you* want to lose weight, it first starts with *you*. To become the best, *you* must start doing your best. Your best starts when you stop holding yourself back from being the best person that you can be.

It will be your personal decisions (choices), actions, and results that will make the difference in your life. When was the last time you mentally, emotionally, spiritually and physically gave yourself the green light to enjoy a better life? Was it today? Was it last week? Last year? Ten years ago? One way to enjoy a better life is to give yourself the permission to enjoy your life daily.

Give yourself the permission to dream bigger dreams, explore new opportunities, and have more fun. Don't place yourself in the same lane with the people who are still sitting at the same red light in their lives. The reason most people continue to remain at the same red light in their lives is because they never give themselves the permission to move forward in their lives. Give yourself the permission to move forward in your life.

If you could make every day "the best day" of your life, would you put forth the effort to make *every day* your best day? If you said yes, why not start doing your "best" today? As of this moment, start giving your *best* effort. You can literally change the quality of your life, once you give yourself the permission to enjoy your life, on a daily basis.

FROM OLD TO NEW

How many people do you know who want to remain at the same level in their lives? Yes, there are a few people who are still at the same level that they were ten years ago. Though they may still be at the same level, nobody wants to keep his or her life docked at the port called "*The same ole, same ole.*"

Many people will continue to live unhappy and unbalanced lives, simply because they don't want to change their lives. They are accustomed to the "old side" of themselves. The *old side* consists of doing the same *old* things, producing the same *old* results, schmoozing with the same *old* people, and going to the same *old* places where nothing changes.

Doing the same *old* things will repeatedly give you the same *old* results in your life. If your *old* results are unsuccessful and they aren't working for you, you can upgrade your results by trying something new. There is nothing wrong with doing new things in life. Doing new things will enable you to start producing new and effective results that will help you succeed. When you want *new* results, you will need to upgrade your *old* results into "new" and "improved" results.

TAKE A LOOK IN THE MIRROR

As the journalist Sydney J. Harris once said, "Ninety percent of the world's woes comes from people not knowing themselves, their abilities, their frailties, and even their real virtues. Most of us, go almost all the way through life as complete strangers to ourselves."

If you were to look at *yourself* in the mirror whom would you see? The answer is obvious–you would see *yourself*. The person *you* see in the mirror will be the person who will ultimately change your life. Don't be afraid or run away from the person that you see in the mirror. Begin to applaud the person that you see in the mirror. Why would you want to become a fugitive from yourself? *Who* are you running away from? *What* are you running away from? *Where* are you running?

Did you know the majority of the children who runaway from home, don't runaway from home because something *bad* happened to them? Many kids runaway from home because they are *confused* about what is happening or not happening in their homes.

Many people attempt to hide their internal confusion from others, as well as from themselves. For example, some people try to drink their internal confusion away by constantly drinking alcoholic beverages, which is not an effective solution. *Internal confusion* is common among people throughout the world. Regardless if you're rich or poor, woman or man, adult or teenager, we all have internal confusion. We must all seek answers to resolve our own confusion. There is nothing wrong with seeking solutions. When you seek solutions, you will get a better understanding how to overcome your internal confusion.

The following are a few examples of *internal confusion* that countless people are seeking solutions for:

- Why did my stock lose money?
- How can I make more money?
- How will I pay my rent/mortgage or car note?
- How do I know if he/she really loves me?
- What is my purpose here on earth?
- How can I improve myself and/or my relationship?
- How can I spend more quality time with my family?
- Which person is trustworthy?
- Should I put on the black pair or the red pair of shoes?
- How can I change my life, so I can live a better life?

- Will I succeed or will I fail?
- Why does this always happen to me?
- Why do my parents like my sister/brother more than me?
- What do I have to do to make him/her and myself happy?
- Why did my parents put me up for adoption?
- Who are my real parents? And where are they?
- What do I want to achieve in my life?
- Why am I always feeling this way?

Rather than viewing internal confusion as a bad thing, progress thinkers look for ways to use it to their advantage. As Dr. Shad Helmstetter wrote in his book, *What To Say When You Talk To Your Self*, "Self-Talk changes the picture–it changes the programming, which creates the belief, which develops the attitude, which creates the feelings, which controls the behavior." Internal confusion will compel you to take a personal survey on yourself, which will give you the opportunity to discover new answers. You may be confused at the beginning, but the more questions that you ask yourself, the more you will discover new solutions to the answers that you're seeking.

THE MIRROR REFLECTION OF "WHY ME?"

It's been said, "The true battlefield is within." There are countless people who are afraid to look at themselves in the mirror, not necessarily because they are afraid of the mirror, but mainly because of what took place in their *past*.

For many people, something "confusing" or "drastic" occurred in their past. In the past, during their adverse time they would usually look at themselves in the mirror and ask the question, "Why is this happening to me?" For example, the person who was molested at a young age would ask himself or herself, "Why is this happening to me?" The drug addict who wants to desperately kick the drug habit asks, "Why is this happening to me?" The person who was constantly compared to his or her siblings found oneself inquiring, "Why is this happening to me?" The person who could never please or prove oneself to his or her parents would go to the mirror and ask, "Why is this happening to me?" The unemployed mother or father who wants to provide a better living for his or her family asks, "Why is this happening to me?" There are countless scenarios that could be included when it comes to the topic "Why me?"

The "Why me?" question has entered into every person's mind, at least once. Some people try to place their *old hurt* behind them by not looking at themselves in the mirror. Why? Because during their painful past experience the only friend they had at that moment was the person in the mirror. Looking into the mirror continues to reflect the "old pain" and "internal confusion" of how things *used to be*. If this has happened to you, you're not alone. Even though the occurrence might have happened in your *past*, you may still see the person you *used to* see in the mirror during those painful times. Due to the pain you went through in your past, looking into the mirror in the present tense may have become a hard task for you, so hard that you still have difficulties facing yourself in the mirror.

> *"You gain strength, courage and confidence by every experience in which you really stop to look fear in the face. You are able to say to yourself, 'I have lived through this horror. I can take the next thing that comes along.' You must do the thing you think you cannot do."*
> –ELEANOR ROOSEVELT

When challenges occur, tell yourself, "This too shall pass." Trying to duck and dodge a challenge won't get you around it. When you encounter a challenge, the best way to breakthrough it is to face it and take on the challenge. As Eleanor Roosevelt once affirmed, "You gain strength, courage and confidence by every experience in which you really stop to look fear in the face. You are able to say to yourself, 'I have lived through this horror. I can take the next thing that comes along.' You must do the thing you think you cannot do."

When it comes to personal challenges, why would you want to run away from a challenge, when the challenge is not running away from you? You can overcome your challenges, when you face your challenges.

In his book *Think Like A Champion*, Donald Trump stated, "Sometimes people spend too much time focusing on problems instead of focusing on opportunities." As a progress thinker, you can overcome your challenges once you begin to seek opportunities. If "internal confusion" is a challenge for you, remember, you can overcome your challenges. Start looking at the bigger picture, instead of the smaller picture. Start looking forward, rather than looking backwards. Start looking toward the future. From this moment forward, whenever you look in the mirror, look at yourself as a brand new person. The next time you encounter a challenge, simply tell yourself, "This too shall pass."

WHAT BETTER CHOICES CAN DO FOR YOU?

If you visited a restaurant, picked up the menu and looked through it you would see a variety of *choices* available on the menu that you could order inside the restaurant. *Choices* occur every second of our lives. Whether we are looking at a menu inside a restaurant or sitting outside on a park bench our minds are always presented with *choices*. For example, while holding the menu, you have a *choice* to open and order from the menu, or close and don't order from the menu. While sitting on the bench, you have a *choice* to read a book, talk to others, or stand up from the bench.

Keep in mind that your personal decisions will display your personal results. Every choice you make will produce a result in your life. Speaking of choices, when you want to lose weight, it's not the "diet" that will make you lose weight, it's the food you "choose" to eat that will make you lose weight. Better choices will produce better results. When you make better choices, you will produce better results that will enable you to make progress and succeed.

THE "I CAN'T" SYNDROME

How many times have you heard someone say the words, "I can't?" As a progress thinker, you will need to condition your mind to think, "I can" more than "I can't." Why? Because the moment you say, "I can't" that will be the moment you instantly defeat yourself. The words, "I can't" are not only *self-depressing*, but they are also *self-defeating*.

The words, "I can't" have been used so many times that people have literally started to believe it in their sleep. For example, late one night, while a husband and wife slept in their bed. The wife was abruptly awakened, due to a mysterious sound. She quickly sat up and turned on the night lamp on her side of the bed. As she sat up in bed with the light on, she noticed her husband repeating the words, "I can't...I can't."

The wife didn't know if her husband was having a bad dream or if he was talking to her. She didn't know if she should wake him up or let him continue to sleep. After a few seconds, her husband stopped saying the words out loud. A few moments later, the wife turned off the light and went back to sleep.

The next morning, the husband said to his wife, "Honey, I had a bizarre dream last night." The wife asked her husband, "What did you dream about?" As the husband focused his attention inside the *employment section* of the newspaper he said, "I had a dream that I should start my own company."

Although the husband had been downsized from his 9-to-5 job, he mentally and physically refused to give himself the permission to change his personal life and employment circumstances. Without considering the new idea of starting his own company, he simply told himself that he couldn't do it. Instead of welcoming the new vision of starting his own company, he declined the vision with the words, "I can't" because he couldn't see himself owning his own company.

If the husband would have at least considered the thought of launching his own business, he would have noticed that he had the opportunity to set himself up to never get laid-off again. His dream could have been his personal wake-up call to start his own company. Launching his own company would have given him the opportunity to create a job he loved doing, set his own working hours, set his own salary, and create jobs for others. Instead, he refused the new idea by mentally telling himself, "I can't" before ever putting forth the physical effort to start his own company.

Every day there are countless people who quickly tell themselves, "I can't" *before* ever putting forth the physical effort toward what they are saying they cannot do. Rather than putting forth the physical effort toward what they want to achieve, many people tell themselves, "I can't do it."

Using the phrase, "I can't" always causes us to perceive things as being impossible. For example, a person will see a luxury car cruising down the street. The first thought that enters the person's mind is *"I can't* afford to drive a car like that." There are people who will see a nice house. The first thought in their mind is *"I can't* afford a house like that." Have you ever noticed how some people will read an article in a publication about someone famous or wealthy, and then quickly say,

"Wow! That's a lot of money, but *I can't* make a fraction of that amount of money?"

It's the usage of the words, "I can't" that usually cause millions of people to remain at dead-end jobs for twenty plus years. It's the words, "I can't" that keep most people mentally, emotionally, physically, financially, and spiritually broke in their lives. It's the words, "I can't" that cause people to give up on themselves and their dreams. It's the words, "I can't" that will delay your success. It's the words, "I can't" that will keep you dreaming small, when your mind is ready to dream bigger. It's the words, "I can't" that will cause you to defeat yourself, even when you know you *can* win.

The words, "I can't" will cause you to live an unhappy life. Whenever you use the words, "I can't" you will deprive yourself mentally, emotionally, physically, and financially from moving forward and upward in your own life. If you are constantly saying, "I can't" when are you going to start telling yourself, "I can?"

THE NEXT STEP UP FROM "I CAN'T"

If you were to study the wealthy people of today and in the past you would discover that most of them didn't have a lot of money at the beginning, nonetheless, they succeeded in their lives.

There are an abundance of wealthy people who started at the bottom. Some of them only had one or two pair of pants with lent and holes in their pockets before they accumulated their wealth. How did they become wealthy? They gave themselves the permission to succeed. Instead of telling themselves, "I *can't* succeed," they gave themselves the permission to say, "I *can* succeed."

The people who say, "I *can't*" always create more room for the people who say, "I *can*." Besides the money, the main difference between a *rich person* and a *poor person* boils down to two words: "I *can*" and "I *can't*." For example, the wealthy people who used to be poor stopped telling themselves, "I *can't*" and started telling themselves, "I *can*." My life changed when I changed my mental vocabulary. Instead of telling myself, "I *can't* succeed," I started telling myself, "I *can* succeed."

Progress thinkers succeed because they believe in themselves. Successful people always believe they *can and will* succeed. Unsuccessful people always believe they *can't and won't* succeed.

Napoleon Hill, the author of *Think & Grow Rich*, once stated, "Whatever the mind can conceive and believe it can achieve." As a progress thinker, you can do whatever you desire, once you believe and give yourself the permission to achieve it. Whatever you put your mind to achieve, you *can* achieve. You *can* succeed when you take action to succeed. You *can* overcome the adversity, stress, and financial challenges in your life. You *can* move onward from a divorce. You *can* turn your mental dreams into a physical success.

In order for you to elevate your progress to the next level, you must believe that you can and will succeed. When your goal is to succeed, you will need to delete the words "I can't" from your vocabulary. The words, "I can't" will *block* your progress from success. The words, "I can" will *build* your progress toward success. Will you *build* or *block* your own success?

An effective way to conquer the "I can't" syndrome is to start telling yourself, "I can" and "I will." You *can* succeed in anything, once you give yourself the permission to succeed. Give yourself the permission to think bigger and reach for the stars.

Commence to condition your mind with the words, "I *can* succeed" and "I *will* succeed." The more you mentally tell yourself that you "can" and "will" succeed, the more your subconscious mind will begin to absorb it and accept it into your mental vocabulary. This is why it's important to feed your mind with optimistic foods. Your mind must constantly be feed and reminded that "you *can* succeed," so you will mentally and physically succeed. The more you tell yourself that you *can and will* succeed, the higher you will elevate yourself to the next level.

PERMISSION TO WIN THE GAME

A few years ago, someone once told me, "Life is a game. When you learn the rules of the game, you will learn how to win the game of life." At first, I didn't understand the logic behind the statement, until one day the statement finally made sense to me.

The previous quote explains the main reason why many wealthy people continue to get wealthier. Wealthy people have learned the rules of how to make, invest, and save their money, as well as enjoy their lives at the same time. One major rule to the game called *life* is to give yourself the permission to create and enjoy a better life for yourself and your family.

Moreover, it comes from giving yourself the permission to go beyond the person you *used to* be, to becoming the person you really *want to* be. As the late Jim Rohn, author and speaker, once stated, "Set a goal to become a millionaire for what it makes of you to achieve it. Because it's not the money that's really important. What's important is the person you have to become in the process.''

> *"To dream anything you want to that is the beauty of the human mind. To do anything you want to that is the strength of the human will. To trust yourself to test the limits that is the courage to succeed."*
> –LINDSEY SMITH

As Lindsey Smith said, "To dream anything you want to that is the beauty of the human mind. To do anything you want to that is the strength of the human will. To trust yourself to test the limits that is the courage to succeed." To succeed in anything, you will need to go through a process.

One vital element within every process is to gain the courage to trust yourself. Trust your instincts. The famous TV host and media mogul Oprah Winfrey asserted, "Follow your instincts. That's where true wisdom manifests itself." Sometimes your instincts will give you an advance warning before something occurs. Pay attention to your intuition because it will give you insight on who and what to avoid, who are the right people to surround yourself with, what's the best deal, as well as which direction to travel on your journey.

DAILY PERMISSION

Give yourself the permission to be the best person that you can be today and every day. Get in the habit of giving your best performance daily. The time has arrived for you to physically go for what you want to achieve in your life. No more excuses, because you have threw all of your excuses away. Now it's time to go beyond the excuses. How? By simply standing up, putting on your think progress cap and taking a step forward.

You will need to take the first step across the starting line to reach your achievement line. One way to continuously cross your starting line is by conditioning yourself mentally, emotionally and physically to take another step forward. For instance, every morning upon waking, start your day by literally telling yourself <u>one</u> of the following:

- "I am a champion and I am getting better every day."
- "Permission granted to achieve more today."
- "I have given myself the authority to succeed today."
- "Hello world!" (Say it aloud with enthusiasm)
- "I will make today my best day ever."

Using the previous phrases will expand your mental vision and physical action. Likewise, it will give you the opportunity to set the tempo of your day. Stop looking for ways that will *limit* your progress. Start looking for ways that will *extend* and *enhance* your progress.

As Dale Carnegie once stated, "You can make more friends in two months by becoming interested in other people, than you can in two years by trying to get other people interested in you." If you want to expedite your progress, get involved with helping others succeed. Volunteer yourself, your time, and your resources. Give yourself the permission to do something daily that will help others succeed in their lives. When you do something that will improve someone else's life, you will discover the treasure chest that will improve your life.

THE SIZE OF YOUR VISION

There are times when we will need to mentally and physically step away from people, places, and things to focus on the quality of our personal vision, life, and success. There is nothing wrong with spending quality time with yourself. Spending quality time with yourself enables you to gather your thoughts together. Also, it will give you the opportunity to upgrade your mind, actions, results, and life.

Some people think that once someone they know (a friend or a relative) succeeds, that the successful person will leave them behind. For instance, has someone ever said to you, "When you make it big, don't forget about us small people?" The small-minded people need to grow up. Think about it. What progress steps are they taking to better themselves? It may sound harsh, but the same way you're striving to improve and better your life, they can start putting forth the effort to *improve* and *better* their lives too.

The next time someone says, "Don't forget about us small people." Simply ask them, "What *progress steps* are you taking to grow as a person?" Just because the people around you think smaller than you that doesn't necessarily mean you have to belittle or shrink your big vision to their level. If the size of the people around your vision, thoughts, and actions doesn't measure up to yours, that may be an indication that it's time for you to upgrade yourself and the people around you. As progress thinkers and action takers, we must become the leaders and examples that will show others how to *think bigger* and *achieve more* in life.

Unsuccessful people remain *small* mentally, emotionally, physically, and financially simply because they mentally view themselves as being *small*. Successful people refuse to think of themselves as *small* thinkers and doers. Though successful people pay attention to the *small* details, they continue to focus on their *big* picture, which consists of the goals that they are aiming to achieve.

As a progress thinker, it doesn't matter the height you are on the outside. What does matter is the height you are on the inside of your mind. Give yourself the permission to enlarge your vision to extraordinary heights. Allow your mind to think bigger and aim higher. When you keep your mind and actions focused on achieving your goals, you will reward yourself by physically achieving them.

FEEL GREAT, NOT GUILTY

As Eleanor Roosevelt once said, "Do what you feel in your heart to be right, for you'll be criticized anyway. You'll be damned if you do and damned if you don't." Don't fall into the *feel-guilty* trap, which usually occurs once you accomplish one of your goals, and then feel guilty afterwards because someone else may criticize you for achieving it.

If you like it or not, people will always talk about you regardless of what you do, so why dwell on what people *think* or *say* about you? You can tell people to stop talking about you, but you can't always stop how they think and feel about you. To maximize your progress, you will need to mentally, emotionally, and physically go beyond what people say and/or think about you. Every person wants to be perceived in a good way; however, there are some people who only look for negativity, so they can criticize, scold, and make others look bad. We have all had our embarrassing moments. I have definitely had plenty of embarrassing moments; nevertheless, I refused to allow anything or anyone stop me from achieving my goals.

Napoleon Hill was correct when he said, "Success requires no explanations." As a progress thinker, if someone disapproves or has a problem with you improving your life...tough! They will eventually get over it. Recognize that you have your own life to live, so strive to enjoy your life daily.

There are countless people who don't succeed simply because they refuse to give themselves the permission to succeed. Some people wait for the perfect moment or the perfect person to come along just to give them the permission to succeed. Here is a progress hint for you: Waiting for someone to enter your life just to give you the permission to live and enjoy life is not an effective way to live.

Someone once stated, "If you feel like your life is a seesaw, perhaps you're depending on other people for your ups and downs." We talked about *waiting* a few chapters back. If you're waiting, what are you waiting on? Only *you* will know the correct answer to what you're waiting for in your life. You don't have to wait or ask other people for their permission to live and enjoy your *own* life. Regardless if you're married, divorced or single, you don't have to wait for someone to approve "everything" you do. You are a special person, so start presenting yourself as the V.I.P. that you are. Take pride in who you are and what you stand for.

As a progress thinker, feel *great* about your achievements. Don't feel *guilty* about the things you achieve. Don't trap yourself by feeling guilty for something you worked diligently to achieve. Feel great for your achievements. It was *you* who sacrificed the time and put forth the physical effort to achieve your rewards. Be proud of yourself and your achievements. The more you give yourself permission the faster you will advance your progress, happiness, and achievements. When you strive for the best, you will receive endless rewards in life. Go for what you want to achieve. It will be worth it because you deserve it.

GIVE YOURSELF A STANDING OVATION

One evening, while talking with my friend Carolyn via telephone, I noticed the tone of her voice sounded a little down like she was disappointed about something. I asked Carolyn how was everything going in her life. She said, "Everything is going okay, I just wish my job would improve."

I asked Carolyn what seemed to be her challenge. Her challenge was that she was working long hours at her job, even putting in overtime hours. She didn't mind the overtime hours, but what she disliked was that nobody at her job ever *verbally* thanked her or told her that she had done a great job.

I asked Carolyn, "When was the last time you gave yourself a standing ovation?" She responded with, "Skip, are you kidding me? Why would I want to give myself a standing ovation?" I calmly said to her, "Why would you want to give another person power over your life?" There was silence on the phone. I stated to Carolyn, "Stop waiting for someone to tell you *when* you've done a good job. If you're constantly waiting on people to tell you *if* and *when* you've done a good job you will always be disappointed because every person won't tell you what you want to hear."

Then I stated to Carolyn, "There will always be people around you who will look for the bad things you do. Don't focus on them. Place your focal point on the good things you accomplish. *You* and *only you* will truly know when you've made an accomplishment." In conclusion, I told Carolyn, "You're already a special person. Now, you must become the strong person who will stand up and tell yourself when you've done a great job."

The next time Carolyn and I talked via telephone, I noticed that she was filled with enthusiasm. The tone of her voice was upbeat. She explained to me how she gave herself a *standing ovation* at her job.

After working long hours to successfully complete a particular project deadline for her company, Carolyn literally stood up at her cubicle desk and started clapping her hands together. Though her co-workers looked at her in a perplexed manner, she continued to give herself a standing ovation. When her boss approached her, he said, "What are you doing?" Once Carolyn stopped clapping her hands, she said to her boss, "Since no one else seems to notice when I do a great job around here, I decided I would give myself a standing ovation for the great job that I have done here."

Carolyn said her boss stood in front of her with his mouth wide open in an awe mode. Then, he just walked away from her speechless. The next day, Carolyn's boss started looking for various reasons to verbally applaud her by thanking her, and telling her how much of a great job she was doing at the company.

It's amazing how we can go to Broadway plays and sporting events, and give others a standing ovation for *their* performance; yet, many of us neglect to give ourselves a standing ovation for our *own* performance. When was the last time you stood up and gave yourself a standing ovation for something you achieved? Don't wait for someone else to tell you, "Good job." Start telling yourself, "I did a good job" or "Job well done." Sometimes you need to give yourself a pat on the back. Whenever you achieve tasks reward yourself with a standing ovation. Once you complete your tasks, simply stand up and give yourself a standing ovation. While standing and clapping your hands, tell yourself, "Bravo, I did a great job!" As a progress thinker, start giving yourself permission to applaud yourself more because you deserve it.

11

YOU KNOW MORE THAN YOU THINK YOU KNOW

*"The question to ask is not whether you are
a success or failure, but whether you are
a learner or a non-learner."*
–BENJAMIN BARBER

What did you *learn* today? As human beings, we have been learning all of our lives, every since we were babies. When it comes to learning, there are some adults who have chosen to stop learning because they think they don't need to learn anything else. Have you ever noticed how a number of people will see or hear something, then they will quickly say, "I already *know* that" or "I've heard all of this stuff before?" Yet, the same people seem to never apply what they supposedly already knew and have heard before. Learning is a daily process, even when you think you already know all the answers. Keep in mind even the smartest person in the world doesn't know all the answers.

Progress thinkers are life-long learners. They are constantly seeking the knowledge that will show them how to elevate to the next level. As a progress thinker, you will need to do the same. The more you continue to elevate yourself to the next level, the more you will succeed. When was the last time you rewarded yourself with *knowledge*? Knowledge within itself is a reward. Rather than looking for material ways to reward yourself, get in the habit of rewarding yourself by learning something new daily.

Every day is a learning day, which means you can learn something brand new every single day. With all of the innovative technology, access to the Internet, and the resources that we have today, there is an abundance of new information available to us 24 hours a day.

Don't trap your mind with limiting thoughts by thinking that you don't have what it takes to succeed, because you do have what it takes to be successful. The key to progress and success is not to *limit* your mind and knowledge, but to *enhance* your mind with knowledge. Regardless if you have a Ph.D. or no degree, you can enhance your knowledge and succeed. Don't make the mistake of assuming you or anyone else "knows it all." Take advantage of the many resources you have at your disposal and learn something new daily.

KNOWING, PLANNING, AND ACTION

The majority of high achievers know exactly what they want to achieve. This is one reason why most achievers set goals for themselves, because they know having goals will push and challenge them to take action until they achieve their goals.

One of the most effective ways to succeed in anything is to first know "what" you want to achieve. Simply knowing *what* you want to achieve will do more than begin the process, it will advance you one step closer to physically achieving your goals. It will be your *knowing, planning,* and *physical actions* that will place you on the path to success. As a progress thinker, fine-tune your focus, and *know* what you want to achieve. Develop a game *plan* that will enable you to achieve your goals. Continue to take *physical action* toward your plan and goals, until you achieve them.

YOU DON'T HAVE TO KNOW EVERYTHING

We live in a society where people are constantly placing emphasis on the belief that every person must know "everything" in his or her life in order to be successful. This myth alone has caused a multitude of people to stop striving to succeed in their lives.

There are people who actually think and believe they have to know *everything* in order for them to succeed. Unfortunately, in their minds if they don't know everything or if they don't fully comprehend an idea or grasp a certain skill, they tend to get stressed. If you don't understand something, don't stress yourself out about it. Simply research what you don't know or ask someone who does know the answers that you are seeking.

There are people who don't succeed because they stop striving to succeed. Underachievers usually *stop* their actions before they physically *start* their actions. Then, they ask themselves, "Why am I not succeeding?" When you think that you have to know everything at the beginning stage you will neglect to maximize your potential toward what you want to achieve. The myth about having to know everything has either slowed down or stopped countless people from achieving their dreams and goals. Don't let this happen to you. You might not know "everything" at the beginning, but you must be willing to open your mind to learn new concepts.

Do you think the Wright Brothers' knew *everything* when they first built the Kitty Hawk? No, the Wright Brothers' didn't know everything at the beginning, but they kept researching and fine-tuning their discoveries along the way. Today, there are various airplanes (including private jets) flying all around the world. Do you think Bill Gates and Paul Allen knew *everything* when they created the *Microsoft* software? No, but they kept researching and revamping their software until they succeeded. Do you think Nora Roberts knew *everything* about writing novels the first time she sat down to type her book? No, but Nora kept typing and improving her creativity to the point that her bestselling novels continue to sell off the shelves

> *"Not all learning comes from books. You have to live a lot."*
> –LORETTA LYNN

Every person knows something. However, nobody knows *everything*, not even the person who is labeled as a "genius." As the country music singer, songwriter, and author, Loretta Lynn once stated, "Not all learning comes from books. You have to live a lot." At the beginning, you don't have to know *every* single detail. But, it's good to know enough to start the momentum. Most successful people learn how to succeed "on" their journey, not before their journey.

The world is always changing, so if you try to learn "everything" *before* you start, you will quickly learn that some of the things you learned–at the beginning–will be obsolete *after* you start. This is why it's essential to keep *learning* something new daily, because what you learned yesterday may be outdated today. Every day strive to learn more than you did yesterday and last week. The more you learn, the more you will stay ahead of the game.

LEARN THE FUNDAMENTALS

The majority of achievers and leaders who have reached greatness, success, wealth, and made history didn't know *everything* when they first started out, yet they succeeded. You may be asking, "How is that possible?" It's possible because they learned the fundamentals of what they wanted to achieve. Then, they placed their mental and physical focal point on achieving their ultimate goals. As a progress thinker, learning the fundamentals is essential because it will teach you how to begin, play, win, and thrive in your endeavors.

In his book called *Succeeding Against The Odds*, Mr. John H. Johnson, the founder of Ebony and Jet magazine, described in detail how he successfully built his empire. When Mr. Johnson first started his magazine publishing company, he disclosed that he didn't know everything about publishing and editing magazines. Though Mr. Johnson didn't know everything at the beginning, he continued to seek innovative resources to make his company successful. Also, John H. Johnson started his dream with $500 dollars, which he borrowed from his mother to launch his own magazine publishing company into a multi-million dollar empire.

Once you start, you may not know "everything." Nonetheless, you can begin the process of learning how to elevate your success. To succeed, you will need to do your homework on what you want to achieve. For example, if your dream is to buy a *Mercedes-Benz*, start researching the class and series you want to buy. Do you want the S, C, E, SL, CL, or M-*Class*? Do you want a two or four-door? How much does the car cost? What features are standard and optional? What colors are available? When do you want to purchase the car? These are simple questions, but they are necessary to get a better understanding of what you want. One of the best ways to get a better understanding is by starting with the fundamental questions.

In his book *Create Your Own Future*, Brian Tracy wrote, "When you learn what you need to learn, and then apply that knowledge, the achievement of your goal becomes almost inevitable." The secret to making progress is to "learn and apply" what you learn. Learning and applying the fundamentals is the core secret for every success. As a progress thinker, it's imperative to first learn the basics of what you want to achieve. Then, implement and improve what you learned from the basics.

THIS IS ALL I KNOW SYNDROME

Every day I get the opportunity to meet new people. While conversing, I have started to notice whenever someone uses the phrase, "This is all I know" it usually follow the words, "I can't." For instance, people habitually say, "I *can't* do that because *this is all I know*."

As progress thinkers, we know more than we think we know. We have too much potential within us to limit ourselves to one level in our lives. For example, there are intelligent and hard working employees who continue to settle for *less* than they are worth. Some of them earn near or less than $30,000 a year. Yet, they refuse to excel beyond their annual income, because they are *used to* earning the same amount per year. Why does this happen? Because they have allowed their minds to accept the thought of "This is all I am supposed to earn."

This reminds me of a story that I once heard the late Jim Rohn talk about. In his story, Jim Rohn described how he showed his mentor a paycheck that he had received from his employer. From the look on Mr. Rohn's face, his mentor knew something was wrong, so he asked Mr. Rohn what was wrong. So, Mr. Rohn showed his paycheck to his mentor. Then, Mr. Rohn stated, "This is all the company pays." The response from his mentor was priceless. His mentor replied, "This is not all that the company pays. This is all that the company pays *you*."

Having a "this is all I know" mentality has kept millions of people working at the same job and remaining at the same level for years. Though many people *know* deep within themselves that they have the potential to do more with and in their lives, they refuse to adventure into doing something new or different in their lives. Why? Because they have conditioned their minds to believe the words, "This is all I know." Whenever you tell yourself, "This is all I know" you will not only limit yourself from *learning* more, you will limit yourself from *achieving* more. When you want to hoist yourself to new heights, you must be willing to learn and achieve more.

One Saturday afternoon, I was talking with a friend name E.J. In the midst of our conversation, I told E.J., "Just because you have worked at the same company for many years, doing the same thing over and over, doesn't mean that is all you are supposed to do with your life." Remember, you know more than you think you know. There are plenty of places that you can go, people you can see, and dreams you can achieve, rather than stare at one tree your entire life. In other words, don't limit yourself to *only* one thing. Give yourself the permission to extend yourself beyond your comfort zone, so you can explore and accomplish more in your life.

Knowledge and progress is like a checkerboard game. It doesn't matter what color your checkers – red or black – it's always your move. Make your move. Begin to take advantage of the knowledge that is available to you. Read books, ask people questions, take notes, and take action.

THE RESULTS OF THIS IS ALL I KNOW

A few years ago, when I started my own company, Skip Williams Communications, I was asked to participate in a job fair event. I was so thrilled to be there that I didn't stand behind the table like everyone else. I stood in *front* of my table. As I conversed with numerous attendees about how they could create a better life for themselves, I remember one particular gentleman who stood out from the rest. As he approached my table, I smiled and said "Hello Sir. How are you doing on this productive day?" He replied, "Um, hi, I'm not doing." With his feeble response, I wanted to dig deeper to see what was wrong, and see how I could help him produce better results in his life.

So, I asked the gentleman, "Did you find a job that interested you today?" Without answering my question, he started complaining about how there were too many people at the event. He complained about how the company that he previously worked for had just released him after being employed at the company for eleven years. I empathized with the gentleman because no one wants to get fired from his or her job. After listening to the gentleman, I inquired, "Sir, have you ever thought about starting your *own* company?" He looked at me as though I had stepped on his last cookie. In a detestable tone, he uttered, "No! And I will never think about it." In conclusion, with his voice raised a few notches higher,

"I have always worked for someone else because *that's all I know* how to do." Then, he walked away from my table.

There are countless people who are just like that gentleman at the job fair. Instead of looking for a better way to change and enjoy their lives, many people would rather *complain* about how bad their lives are going. One reason people choose to complain is because that's all they know how to do. The second reason people complain is because they are afraid to change or they don't know what to change, so they complain about it.

As a progress thinker, don't strive to be a complainer. Strive to create a better life for yourself and your family. You can accomplish more once you stop holding yourself back. Keep in mind there is always room to learn something new. Instead of thinking and saying, "This is all I know," start aiming higher to learn something new. Study successful people. Seek the best people with the most effective and resourceful information. Ask them questions. Read up-to-date books and magazines in your field. Eliminate the thought of "this is all I know," because you can always learn more. Open your mind to new ideas. Diversify the people, places, and things around you. Learning and applying these simple and effective strategies will give you the opportunity to learn more, so you can accomplish more in your endeavors.

WHAT ELSE DO YOU KNOW?

You may have just won an award or a championship. You might be a newlywed or have been married for years. You could have a million dollars in your bank account or a penny in your pocket, despite what you have accomplished thus far there is always room for *improvement* and *change* in your life.

When some of us hear the word *change*, the first thought that automatically enters our mind is, "I *can't* do that because *this is all I know* what to do in my life." Don't *cheat* yourself; *create* yourself. Like I've stated to my clients, "It's <u>not</u> all you know. It's all you <u>choose</u> to know." If you're a "This is all I know" person, take a moment to ask yourself, "What else do I know?"

Rather than limiting yourself with "This is all I know" commence to *expand your knows*. Yes, you may have worked at the same company for years; however, did you *know* that you could take the knowledge, skills, and experience that you've gained from the company you work at, and launch your own company? Did you *know* that you have the ability to move upward to a higher position within the company you are currently working at? Did you *know* there is a gift within you that is ready to be opened? Did you *know* success has your name on it? Did you *know* there are various accomplishments you can achieve in life? Did you *know* that you could literally create and build multiple streams of income to increase your current finances? If you wanted to, did you *know* that you could change your professional career and personal life? Did you *know* there are countless books that you can read to increase your *know*ledge? Did you *know* that you have access to professional, creative, and wealthy people who can and who are willing to assist you with your ideas? Did you *know* that you could literally advance your progress, life, and success?

Overall, there are too many resources of people, information, books, audio programs, seminars, and Internet access available for you to say...

- "I don't know."
- "This is all I know."
- "This is all I am supposed to know."

As Sudie Back once stated, "Be curious always! For knowledge will not acquire you; you must acquire it." I concur. This is one of the main reasons why I'm always reading and researching, because my mind is filled with curiosity and is thirsty to learn something new. The only way to quench my mental thirty is by feeding it with more valuable knowledge. Every person can expand his or her own *knows*, including you. Just because you've worked at the same job for years, have done the same tasks the same way for years, been married to the same person for years, been emotionally and/or financially broke for years doesn't mean you cannot expand your personal and professional *knows*. There is always room available for you to upgrade what you currently *know*. The secret to knowledge: You must be willing to *learn* and *know* more.

The legendary author Mark Twain once declared, "The man who doesn't read good books has no advantage over the man who can't read them." It doesn't matter if you are a man, woman, or teenager there is plenty of *know*ledge available for you to learn and gain from it. Research studies have shown once people leave school – high school and/or college – they rarely read books. They may read one book within the entire year. Think about it. Most adults wake up, take a shower, get dressed and go to work. They arrive home, look at TV, spend time with their husband/wife and/or children, take a shower or bath, and go to sleep. Then, wake up the next day, just to do the *exact* same thing over and over again for the rest of their lives.

You can *change* your life, once you remove your "This is all I know" limits. Life is constantly changing every day. To get ahead, you will need to learn more to get ahead and stay ahead. Whatever you want to achieve seek the knowledge for it daily. The more knowledge you gain, on a daily basis, the faster you will learn how to achieve your ultimate goals.

LEARN UNTIL YOU KNOW

When I was growing up, I didn't read a lot of books. Like many people, I used to neglect reading books. My niche for reading books occurred in the midst of my hardships, when I was financially broke and living in a boarding house, which I previously mentioned in Chapter 7 (School of Hard Knocks). I didn't get serious about reading until I read a few books that opened my mind to new ideas.

It was books such as *Think and Grow Rich* by Napoleon Hill, *Think Like A Winner* by Dr. Walter Doyle Staples, *How to Stop Worrying and Start Living* by Dale Carnegie, *Psycho-Cybernetics* by Maxell Maltz and *Awaken The Giant Within* by Anthony Robbins that enhanced my interest to want to read more books. While reading books, I began to learn a variety of new strategies that helped me improve my life. The more I learned how to improve my life, the more I wanted to read more books. I went from <u>not</u> reading books to literally "writing" books.

You can produce new results, when you have an open mindset. Reading mind-worthy books will give you the knowledge to grow in any area of your life. Within my life, reading diverse books such as The Bible, self-help, personal finance, business, motivational, psychology, and autobiographies helped me gain the knowledge I needed to prevail personally and professionally.

As a progress thinker, you will learn more once you allow your mind to inquire, "What does this mean?" Open your mind to new ideas and you will be amazed at the outcome. An effective way to make progress is by deleting the "no's" out of your life, and start welcoming the "knows" into your life. For example, stop telling yourself, "*No*, I can't succeed." Instead, start telling yourself, "I *know* that I can and I will succeed."

The key to progress and success is to open your mind to new concepts. When you have an open-mind, you will discover the doors to new opportunities. Opportunities are everywhere. Once you open your mind and expand your *knows*, you will begin to see and encounter more opportunities on your journey.

Learning is endless. You have the opportunity to advance your knowledge every single day. Why not put forth the effort to learn more, so you will *know* more? Read publications that will enhance your skills, and that will stretch your mind to think more creatively. If you already *know* something, strive to upgrade your *know*ledge. Instead of thinking and saying, "This is all I *know* in my life." Start thinking and saying, "I want to *know* more in my life!"

TURN ON YOUR PC

Did you know your mind is a personal computer with unlimited capacity? You are the official owner of your own personal computer with unlimited creativity.

As human beings, we never truly reach our full *mental* capacity. Why? Because there is always room available for our minds to learn new, more, and valuable information. Our minds are designed with unlimited access to explore new ways to succeed. For example, you can *program* your mind to succeed. You can *upgrade* our mind. You can *upload* and *download* the latest data (information), and *delete* the outdated data. The great thing about your *mental* PC is that it's portable. You can physically take your *mental* PC anywhere and everywhere that you want go.

The majority of successful people who reach success started with a big *mental* vision. High achievers turn on, keep on, and constantly use their mental PCs. They are always focusing on their big vision, which is usually what they want to physically accomplish.

As a progress thinker, remember that your mind is a valuable personal computer. Turn on your mental PC and start using it productively. Don't just download "anything" into your mind. Always look for creative ways to upgrade your mind with "new" and "effective" *mental* data that will enhance your mind, actions, progress, wealth, and success.

12

MISSION IS POSSIBLE

"It's kind of fun to do the impossible."
–WALT DISNEY

As kids, most of us heard the story about how Jack jumped over the candlestick. In the story, when Jack jumped over the candlestick, the *impossible* thought of not making it over the candlestick never crossed Jack's mind, because he believed it was *possible*. As a result, Jack successfully jumped over the candle.

As a progress thinker, you will encounter a few challenges on your journey, but that's not a reason to give up. Despite which paths you take there will be challenges. Why? Because challenges come with the territory. When challenges occur on your journey each one will test your belief system to see how strong you believe in what you're out to achieve. Do you *believe* your goals and dreams are "possible" or "impossible" to achieve? The previous question is where you are presently standing because it's the starting line to everything you want to achieve. This one question will constantly challenge you every step that you take in your endeavors.

Progress thinkers constantly go beyond the word impossible. Nothing is impossible to the person who believes in the *possibility*. We achieve what we *believe is possible* to achieve. In other words, when you believe something is *possible*, you believe it's *achievable*. As a progress thinker, you can physically achieve your goals, ideas and dreams, once you *believe* they are achievable.

BELIEVE IN THE VISION

Within every success story you will see countless people who *believed* in themselves. Success doesn't come easy; however, the people who believe in themselves and who are willing to take action towards what they believe in will prosper in their endeavors.

Howard Schultz, the Chairman, CEO, and the visionary leader of *Starbucks* coffee believed in himself and his vision. Rather than staying local in the Seattle, Washington area, Howard looked at the bigger picture, which was to expand the *Starbucks* brand. His vision entailed more than just selling coffee; he wanted to provide an innovative experience that would make each customer feel welcomed and comfortable.

In his book *Pour Your Heart Into It: How STARBUCKS Built a Company One Cup at a Time*, Howard Schultz stated, "It's more than great coffee. It's the romance of the coffee experience, the feeling of warmth and community people get in *Starbucks* stores." On a daily basis, over 2 million people walk around with *Starbucks* coffee cups in their hands. Today, Howard Schultz's vision for *Starbucks* has become a global brand.

What is your vision of success? What do you see yourself achieving in the next five years? As a progress thinker, you will need to believe in your vision. Imagine yourself achieving your goals. Everything you want to achieve starts in your mind. Your mind is the steering wheel to your decisions, beliefs, actions, and results. Decide what you want to achieve. Believe you will achieve it. Take action toward your vision every day. You must believe in yourself enough to take the first step toward what you want to achieve. Once you mentally take the first step, you will start the momentum that will lead you to the path of prosperity.

COURAGE TO BELIEVE

Every champion has the courage to believe that he or she will succeed. It's the combination of their belief and courage that push them to physically go for what they want to achieve. Champions have dreams and goals just like you. Champions are human just like you. Champions have fears just like you. Champions make mistakes just like you. So what's the distinction between you and champions? The ultimate difference is the courage to take the next step. Champions get knocked down and encounter adversity just like you, but they are courageous enough to get back up and keep moving onward.

One of the most challenging parts about success is gaining the *courage* to succeed. There are countless people who don't succeed, simply because they don't have the *courage to believe in themselves.* We succeed when we gain the *courage* to *believe* in ourselves. The nucleus to every success is to *believe.* As a progress thinker, you must be willing to *believe in yourself* 24 hours a day, seven days a week, and 365 days. You must believe in yourself when times get hard. You must believe in yourself, even when nobody else believes in you.

When you enhance your courage to take action toward your ideas, dreams, and goals, you will double your possibility rate to achieve them. The more you believe in yourself, the more you will gain the courage to build the bridge to your own success.

THE RIGHT ATTITUDE

A positive thinker will always seek and discover a better way to produce successful results. When you think optimistically, you will begin to make more progress. The more progress you make, the faster you will achieve your goals.

If you told people that one day you were going to be famous and earn millions of dollars, they would probably laugh and quickly tell you, "That's impossible." If you think it's impossible, ask the movie star Jim Carrey.

When Jim Carrey first started out as an actor, he told people that he would become famous and make millions of dollars. Many people didn't believe him, while others hysterically laughed at him. Today, Jim Carrey is a movie star and earns $20 million dollars in every movie that he stars in. Who got the last laugh? Jim Carrey got the last laugh. He continued to believe in himself, even when the naysayers didn't believe in him. He kept moving forward and upward on his own success ladder.

If you think your dreams and goals are impossible, think about the numerous successful people who have already achieved their dreams and goals. If others have succeeded, so can you. Now, do you still think your goals and dreams are *impossible* to achieve?

Progress starts with a positive mindset. When you have a positive mental attitude your success will be endless. The right attitude attracts the right opportunities. You can change your negative thoughts into positive thought. You can transform your impossible thoughts into possible thoughts. Instead of focusing on *negative* outcomes, start focusing your mind on *positive* outcomes.

DON'T CUT DOWN THE TREE BEFORE IT GROWS

Mark Twain once said, "Keep away from people who try to belittle your ambitions. Small people always do that, but the really great make you feel that you too, can become great."

One evening, while attending an event in New York, I met two women who were friends. During our conversation, we mostly talked about life. While talking, one of the ladies said to me, "I heard you are an author of a book." Before I could respond, she quickly told me how she wanted to write a book about successful single mothers.

As we talked about the idea of her writing a book, her friend attempted to cut down her idea by stating, "What can you tell people that will make them want to listen to you?" She replied, "I have a lot of things I could tell single mothers about how they can work a full-time job, take care of their kids, and still enjoy their lives."

Her friend continued by saying, "You don't know the first thing about writing a book." The smile on the potential author's face slowly began to disappear. Before her smile completely vanished, I said, "If your desire is to write a book, I would be honored to assist you with completing it." A smile suddenly reappeared on her face. After talking a little more, I gave her one of my business cards.

Since the two ladies were riding in the same car together, they both thanked me for the conversation, and then they departed. To this day, the potential author has yet to contact me. I guess she let her friend cut down her book idea before she fully planted the seed for it to grow into fruition.

> *"Never be bullied into silence.*
> *Never allow yourself to be made a victim.*
> *Accept no one's definition of your life; define yourself."*
> –HARVEY FIERSTEIN

The actor and playwright, Harvey Fierstein said, "Never be bullied into silence. Never allow yourself to be made a victim. Accept no one's definition of your life; define yourself." When you have an idea there will be people who will attempt to place stop signs, detour signs, and one-way signs in your mind. They will use negative and cutting words like, "You're not smart enough." "You'll never succeed, so why try?" "Your dreams are too big." When your objective is to succeed, don't surround yourself with the people who will talk you "out" of what you want to achieve. Start surrounding yourself with the people who will talk you "into" what you want to achieve.

As a progress thinker, you must enhance your mind, courage, and actions to go for what you want to achieve in life. Never let someone stop you from making progress and achieving your dreams and goals. When you want to turn your dreams into reality, don't let someone talk you out of planting your *ideas* and *success* seeds. Refrain from letting negative thinkers cut down your ideas before they grow. In other words, never let someone chop down your dreams. When someone tells you that your dreams are impossible, simply reply, "Don't tell me it's impossible until *after* I'm finished."

It will be your progress that will create your success. After looking around and seeing all the BIG apples on the tree, a baby apple asked one of the BIG apples, "What do I have to do to get BIG like you?" The BIG apple replied, "You must be willing to blossom." As a progress thinker, are you willing to blossom? Have you planted your success seed, so you can blossom? You must plant your *success seed* for your success to grow. When you have an idea, plant your idea seed with confidence. Plant *what* you want to achieve in your mind and take action to achieve it. When you begin to take action toward *what* you want to achieve, it will eventually grow into fruition.

GO BEYOND THE NEGATIVE THINKERS

Have you ever crossed paths with someone who told you that your dreams were too big for you to handle? If so, you're not alone. On many occasions, I have heard derogatory statements such as, "You're a dreamer," and "You'll never succeed" even from my own family and so-called friends.

As a progress thinker, you will constantly cross paths with negative people who think *impossible* thoughts. In the minds of negative thinkers *everything is impossible*, even their own success. There will always be people who will tell you, "Your dreams are impossible to achieve." Who will you believe? Will you believe the people who never achieved "their own" dreams? Or, will you believe in yourself and achieve "your own" dreams?

The majority of us have encountered some form of negativity, whether it was directed toward us or we happened to be in an area where we saw or heard negativity from others. How do you overcome it? You can conquer it by mentally, emotionally, and physically distancing yourself from *negative* thinking people and *negative* words. You will enhance your progress and success, once you remove yourself from negative people, places, and things. Negative environments will cause you to think negative. This is why it's vital that you stop surrounding (trapping) yourself with negativity, because avoiding negative people, places and things will keep you from falling into *negative* traps.

Negative people will always tell you something negative–that's why they are called "negative thinkers." Don't fall into the negative trap. There is one important lesson you must know about negative thinkers: *A negative thinker's biggest pet peeve is to allow a positive thinker to succeed.* In other words, negative thinkers don't want you to succeed. This is why it's imperative that you keep your distance from the negative thinking people. If you don't keep your distance from negative thinking people, you won't succeed. Why? Because they will do whatever it takes to keep you from succeeding, even if that includes wasting your valuable time. Remember, your mind, time, and actions are too valuable to waste, so use them wisely and productively.

The best results occur when negative thinkers are *not* in the vicinity. As a progress thinker, it's essential that you place yourself around positive thinkers and in optimistic environments because it will keep you from falling into the negative traps.

BEYOND THE IMPOSSIBLE…IT'S POSSIBLE

The people who say, "It's impossible" are equipped with the same *mental* potential, as the people who say, "It's possible." The only difference: One seeks the possibility, while the other *refuses* to seek the possibility. For example, four friends were standing on the same side of a river. Two friends said it was *impossible* to cross the river. The other two said it was *possible* to cross the river. Which group of friends do you think crossed the river? Despite what negative thinkers say about you, keep moving forward and upward, until you achieve your ideas, dreams, and goals.

A clogged mind filled with *impossible* thoughts will weaken the mind with *self-defeating* thoughts. Refrain from clogging your mind with impossible thoughts. Impossible doesn't exist in the mind of progress thinkers. Progress thinkers always look beyond the word *impossible*. There is nothing *impossible* to the person whose mind has absorbed the thought of achieving the *possible*. Progress thinkers are determined and action-oriented people. For example, Bill Gates, Oprah Winfrey, and Michael Dell are all household names. How did they become successful household names? They went beyond the word *impossible* and made their dreams *possible*.

Nothing is impossible when you believe in yourself. Do you focus more on the *impossible* or the *possible*? If you focus more on the *impossible*, could it be because you may be afraid of the *possible*? Or, could it be that when you were growing up, you were repeatedly told, "That's impossible" and the words continue to linger within your mind today?

In his book *Pour Your Heart Into It*, Howard Schultz stated, "It takes courage. A lot of people will try to tell you it's impractical or impossible. They'll tell you to lower your sights. They'll tell you business can't be benevolent." Some people are going to tell you, "Your dreams are too big for your head." "Your dreams are impossible." "You'll never succeed." They will even tell you *not* to go for your big dreams and goals. One reason people will tell you that your dreams are impossible is because they never physically went for or fulfilled their own dreams and goals. Another reason people will tell you that your dreams are impossible is because someone once upon a time told them the same thing.

The majority of people who say, "It's impossible" will be the same people who never tried the so-called, "impossible" themselves. The following are the three main reasons why most people will tell you that something is *impossible*:

1. They have never seen it done before.
2. They never achieved it themselves.
3. They don't want to see *you* achieve it.

When you have big dreams, there will always be some people who won't see the big picture, but that doesn't mean you should shrink or disregard your dreams. Some of the things you want to achieve will be perceived as impossible to a few people, simply because they refuse to think bigger or stretch their minds beyond their own limitations. Don't allow another person's mental limitations stop you from achieving your own goals and dreams. Always remember, anything is possible when you mentally condition yourself to believe "IT'S POSSIBLE!"

WAKE UP YOUR DREAMS

If you have a big dream, it's time to wake up your big dream and physically live it. Your dreams are mental previews of what you can achieve once you physically take action toward them.

Some entrepreneurs believe "sleeping" will place them in debt. They believe if they don't have their money *working for them while they sleep* their wealth will dwindle into debt. Could this be the reason why some people are behind on paying their bills? They would rather stay in bed and sleep the entire day away. My life changed when I learned the difference between "liabilities" and "assets." Sleeping is an *asset*, because we need sleep to rejuvenate our mind and body. However, if you sleep too long, sleeping becomes a *liability*.

> *"A dream is a sleeping success that's ready to be physically awakened."*

If you don't have your game plan together you will keep yourself out of the game. What do you have written down for your game plan? Do you have the word, "Sleep" at the top of your list? Or, do you have "Accomplish my goals" at the top of your list? When you're sleeping nothing gets accomplished. To achieve your dreams and goals, you must mentally and physically wake your dreams up with action. It will be your actions and results that will enable you to physically live your dreams.

A dream is a sleeping success that's ready to be physically awakened. *If you want your dreams to come true, don't sleep.* Of course, you will need the proper rest to invigorate your mind and body, but don't sleep so long that you oversleep and sleep your life away. When you oversleep, you will sleep your life away, which will keep you from being productive in your endeavors. In order for your dreams to come true, you will need to wake up your dreams by constantly putting forth the effort to live your dreams every day.

SEE IT. BELIEVE IT. ACHIEVE IT.

Lewis Cass, the 22nd United States Secretary of State, once said, "People may doubt what you say, but they will believe what you do." One day, two construction workers were having a conversation on their lunch break. One construction worker said to the other, "You are looking at a soon-to-be millionaire." The other construction worker laughed hysterically at what he had just heard. After he finished laughing at his co-worker, he said, "A millionaire! Are you kidding me? What channel are you watching in your head?"

A few years later, the two former co-workers crossed paths again. The construction worker who once stated, "You are looking at a soon-to-be millionaire" had reached the millionaire status. While his former co-worker, who once laughed at his big vision, continued to struggle financially living paycheck-to-paycheck. Although both men once worked at the same job, what do you think separated them from producing the same results? The "size" and "quality" of their *mental vision* and *actions* separated them. While one was thinking small, the other one was thinking bigger.

As I once stated to one of my colleagues, "You may not be able to see what I see. And I may not be able to see what you see. But at the end, you will see exactly what I have been looking at the whole time." The millionaire *physically* showed the non-believer exactly what he was *mentally* looking at the entire time. The millionaire had already *visualized* himself, as a millionaire, while his former co-worker *refused to visualize* at all.

The more you believe in yourself, the more you will do whatever it takes to make your dreams become a reality. As a progress thinker, you must think progress, when others aren't thinking about making progress. While others are thinking small, start thinking bigger. Dream BIG! Dream GIGANTIC! But, whatever you do, never let someone deter you from living your own dreams. You can *mentally* and *physically* achieve your own dreams and goals.

"You may not be able to see what I see. And I may not be able to see what you see. But, at the end, you will see exactly what I have been looking at the whole time."

Everything you want to achieve in your *life* begins with what you want to achieve in your *mind*. When you *visualize* what you want to achieve, *believe* in what you want to achieve, *take action* toward what you want to achieve, you will physically achieve it. The secret formula to every success: Never stop taking action toward what you want to achieve.

Your success starts with your vision and actions. When you combine your vision and actions together, you will create your success. When it comes to vision and action, a great example would be Walt Disney. Walt Disney *mentally visualized* the success of Disneyland before it was *physically* created. His belief and vision turned his dream into a successful reality. Today, the Walt Disney Company and Disneyland is a household name worldwide.

Your success is only a vision away. What are you looking at in your mind? What is your vision? Are you envisioning yourself succeeding or failing? Do you see yourself at the next level or remaining at the same level? What do you see yourself achieving today? Tomorrow? Ten years from now? Imagine yourself succeeding. To create your own success, you must *visualize* yourself succeeding. To achieve your own goals, you must foresee yourself achieving your goals. In order to achieve your vision, you must concentrate on achieving your vision. Believe *in* your vision. Most importantly, take action toward your vision every day.

AIM HIGHER, NOT LOWER.

Whatever action you take in life, people will always talk about you. If you do the *right* thing, people will talk about you. If you do the *wrong* thing, people will talk about you. If you do *nothing at all*, people will still find a way to talk about you.

Since you know people are going to talk about you, give them something exciting to talk about. In the words of Henry David Thoreau, "In the long run, men hit only what they aim at. Therefore, they had better aim at something high." When it comes to progress, a persons gender doesn't matter. Regardless if you're a man or a woman, you can aim higher.

Setting higher standards for yourself will be more rewarding than lowering your standards just to say, "I achieved something in life." High achievers succeed because they perpetually set higher standards for themselves to achieve. Every day high achievers–mentally and physically–take action toward their high standards.

There are a few people who would rather laugh at everyone else with a vision because they lack their own vision. *Low achievers* have a hard time succeeding, simply because they lack their own vision. Low achievers have a difficult time succeeding because they wander through life *without* a vision.

Whatever direction your mind aims toward, your actions will follow. Which direction are you aiming? Are you aiming low or high? AIM HIGH! Set higher standards for yourself. You will be amazed at what you will achieve once you direct your actions to move in the direction of your new and higher standards.

CREATE YOUR OWN POSSIBILITIES

If you have made it this far in the book, Congratulations! You have taken the definite step of a champion to create a better life for yourself. While countless people continue to stop themselves at the *impossible*, you have decided to *go beyond the impossible*.

Every *impossible* thought has a *possible* link attached to it. After deleting the *impossible* thoughts from our minds, the next step is to create and build on top of our *possible* thoughts. Anything is possible when you create your own possibility. For example, naysayers told Wilber and Orville Wright – The Wright Brothers – that the Kitty Hawk airplane was impossible. The Wright brothers disregarded the negative input from all the non-believers, also known as the *naysayers*, and made it possible.

There were countless naysayers who didn't believe in the Wright brother's vision. Nevertheless, Wilber and Orville worked diligently by persistently experimenting, until they made the airplane possible. They created their own *possible*, while everyone else thought it was *impossible*. Today, the Wright brother's vision continues to live on, as various airplanes fly all over the world.

> *"When you think positive, have a game plan,*
> *take physical action, and challenge yourself to produce*
> *effective results nothing is impossible."*

Progress thinkers do whatever it takes to achieve their goals. To succeed, your mind must *see, absorb,* and *plan* for your forthcoming success. When you take action toward your mental vision, you will create your own physical success. You don't have to desperately try to fit into someone else's circle to become successful. Create your own success circle. You don't have to stress yourself out because someone doesn't believe in your vision. Just make sure *you* believe in your vision. Do like the Wright Brothers–stand up for what you believe in.

When you think positive, have a game plan, take physical action, and challenge yourself to produce effective results nothing is impossible. Keep in mind, anything is possible when your confidence level is high, and you apply action toward the possible. Lift your head up, put your feet on the ground, and go for what you want to achieve. The mission you want to achieve is always *possible*, once you create your own possibilities.

SUCCESS DOESN'T HAVE LIMITS

There are countless laws and rules throughout the world that notify us what we can and cannot do. However, out of all the rules and laws, I have yet to see or hear of one that states, "A person is prohibited from thinking big and succeeding in his or her life." Why? Because such laws and rules don't exist, which means you have the opportunity to achieve whatever your heart desires. As a progress thinker, you set the laws and rules for your own personal progress and success.

Thinking is FREE. It doesn't cost you anything to think big. For example, we may have to pay for a bottle of water to quench our thirst, but we don't have to pay to think bigger. In other words, you can think as big as you like and not be charged for it. When you think bigger, you can succeed in anything that you put your mind to achieve. Unleash your mind...think bigger!

When someone utters the words, "You *can't* succeed" ask them to show you the laws and rules that specify, "You are *prohibited* from succeeding in your life." There are no laws or rules that prohibit you from succeeding, because success doesn't have a "limit" attached to it. Nobody can stop you from succeeding in your life, except *you*. Start telling yourself, "I *will* succeed."

There are no stop signs on the road to success. As progress thinkers, we either *stop* ourselves from succeeding or we *drive* ourselves until we succeed. It's our personal limits, laws, and rules that cause us to place limitations on our best performance.

Your success starts with *you*. To make progress, you will need to expand your mind and actions beyond the limits that you have placed upon yourself. When you place yourself *beyond* your personal limits, you will do more than prevail; you will also give your best performance. As a progress thinker, remember, you set the limits, laws, and rules to your own life, progress, and success. The moment you remove your personal limitations, you will instantly become "limitless."

13

BUILD YOUR OWN
SUCCESS MOUNTAIN

*"You see things; and say, 'Why?' But I dream things
that never were; and ask, 'Why not?'"*
–GEORGE BERNARD SHAW

There are various levels to reach success. Of all the levels available to succeed, how do you think most people become successful? I'll give you a hint: The majority of successful people *create their own success mountain*.

Building your success mountain is about creating your own paths to succeed. All high achievers build and climb their personal success mountain–internally and externally–to make it to the top. High achievers go beyond waiting for others to make a path for them. Rather than waiting, progress thinkers develop their own success paths to excel to the top. What paths will you create to reach the top of your own success mountain?

If you enjoy hiking or have never been hiking a day in your life, it's your turn to create your own success mountain. Put on your hiking boots. Now, tell yourself, "No matter what happens along the way, I am going to keep climbing, until I reach the top."

START THE MOMENTUM

When your objective is to achieve your ultimate goals, it's never too early or late to give your best effort. In order to reach one or all of your goals, you first must start moving toward your goals.

Forward motion will produce *forward progress*. Forward progress will lead to your success. Every progress and success begins with *forward motion,* which accumulates into momentum. If you don't start the momentum toward your goals and dreams, you will *stop* your progress, before you *start* your progress. If you're not making progress, you're not moving forward. If you are not moving *forward*, you're either standing still or moving backwards. As a progress thinker, release your brakes, so you can start moving *forward* in your life. The key to progress is to keep moving forward.

> *"The act of taking the first step*
> *is what separates the winners from the losers."*
> –BRIAN TRACY

Brian Tracy, bestselling author and speaker, once stated, "The act of taking the first step is what separates the winners from the losers." If you're waiting to start, what are you waiting for? The longer you delay yourself from *starting*, the longer you will hold yourself back from *succeeding.* Don't delay; start today. Today is the beginning to where you want to go tomorrow. Your success is only a few steps away. Every step you take will lead you *somewhere.* Refusing to take action will lead you *nowhere.*

Confucius once said, "A journey of a thousand miles begins with a single step." To arrive at your destination, you will need to take the initial step toward your destination. Your first step *forward* will start your journey toward your success. Once you take the first step forward, you will place yourself one step closer to achieving your goals. Get excited about achieving your goals. The more progress you make, the faster you will accelerate yourself to the next level.

TWO POPULAR DESTINATIONS

Building your own success mountain will lead you to a variety of destinations. The two most popular destinations that most people strive toward are *happiness* and *success*. These are the two most sought-after destinations in the world.

When it comes to building our own success mountain, *happiness* and *success* are usually placed at or near the top of the list. What is "Happiness" and "Success?" Happiness is an element of pleasure, relief, and joy that generates satisfaction. Success is an extraordinary fulfillment and achievement, which is gained through physical effort and results. Happiness and success is a daily issue. Every day we strive to do things that will make us happy and successful. The following are a few ways some progress thinkers define happiness and success:

• Spending quality time with family, friends, and enhancing networking relationships.
• Having food, clothing, and shelter.
• Losing weight or exercising for a healthier body.
• Setting and accomplishing their goals.
• Freedom to do what they love to do.
• Turning their dreams into reality.

When you strive to *improve* yourself at least one percent, on a daily basis, you will continue to enhance your personal happiness and success daily. For example, if you improve yourself just 1% per day within 30 days you would have improved yourself by 30%. The more you *improve* yourself, the more you will enhance the quality of your results. Keep improving yourself and you will arrive at the world's most popular destinations called *happiness* and *success*.

INTERNAL AND EXTERNAL HAPPINESS

It's been said, "Life isn't about what will make you rich; it's about what will enrich you." Most people categorize success as having large sums of money in their bank accounts, having a luxury car or house, and having various letters before or after their names.

There are successful people who have plenty of money and lavish things to match their wealth and prestige. From the *outside* they are viewed as successful. However, let's take a closer look at this scenario: If a "successful" person had a lot of money, but wasn't internally happy would you continue to call that person *successful?* Take a moment to think about the previous question. Would you label a wealthy person "successful" if he or she were *financially wealthy,* but were *emotionally broke?*

The late Jim Rohn once stated, "How sad to see a father with money and no joy. The man studied economics, but never studied happiness."

There is nothing wrong with having money and nice things just don't allow it to define your happiness. External happiness starts with *internal* happiness. In his book *The 100 Simple Secrets Of Happy People*, David Niven was correct when he wrote, "Happy people let themselves be happy. Unhappy people continue doing things that upset them."

One reason a multitude of people are *unhappy* and *unsuccessful* in their lives is because they are always looking "outside" of themselves for what they already have *inside* of themselves. There are countless people who play hide-n-go seek with themselves, by seeking *outside* of themselves for happiness and success. Many people *find* their happiness. Some people *misplace* their happiness. A few people have yet to discover what makes them happy. Many of us forget to look *within* ourselves for happiness, while in pursuit of external success.

As a progress thinker, remember, happiness and success starts "inside" you. If you're not satisfied with your external results, start working on improving the quality of your "internal" results. Seeking "within" yourself will help you discover your *internal happiness*. Also, it will enable you to become *internally* and *externally* successful.

THE GAME PLAN TO SUCCESS

What is *Success*? This is a question that is constantly being asked. Success is whatever you want it to be. When it comes to *success*, you are the dictionary that defines your own success.

There are people who define their success by being able to see a brand new day. For some, success means having access to millions of dollars in their bank account. Some people define success by being able to eat at least one meal per day.

Today, the word "success" has gotten so out of hand that people are walking around in the daytime with a flashlight looking for their *success*. They are seeking high and low, as well as very hard for the small, yet powerful word called *success*. There are people who have extended their search for success by looking underneath rocks, over fences, and around the world for it. There are a few people who believe success is going to physically come to their doorstep, ring their doorbell, and hand them a package with the words, "Handle With Care Because Your *Success* is Inside!" Success is not going to physically knock on your door, until you knock on its door first.

Every success starts with a game plan. You will begin to make more progress toward success once you create your game plan to succeed. Set your goals, and make a game plan to achieve your goals. What will you achieve today? Write down your daily game plan the night before. Start your day early. Set your alarm clock 30 minutes earlier than you usually start your day. When you start your day 30 minutes early, you will give yourself a head start to achieve more tasks on your to-do list.

THE AROMA OF SUCCESS

Success is like a buffet line full of the world's most delicious gourmet dishes. It has an aroma that makes you want more of it. As a progress thinker, you are the ultimate decision maker that decides what you want to place on your success plate.

Success has a large variety for you to choose from. Keep in mind, like most buffet lines, success is *self-service*, which means no one will bring it to you on a silver platter. In other words, when it comes to success, you must mentally and physically get up, and go for what you want to achieve in your life. What will you put on your success plate today?

USE YOUR OWN SUCCESS RULER

The author Jacqueline Briskin once declared, "Don't take anyone else's definition of success as your own." I concur. When people ask me how they can succeed, I tell them, "Always measure your success with your *own* success ruler, and not by other people's rulers."

Don't let yourself get trapped or sidetracked by what most people label as *success*. Your definition of *success* may differ from others, simply because you have your own vision of success. Your success ruler may be longer than someone else's success ruler, simply because you think bigger than them. For example, while some people are aiming to achieve *small* things in their lives, your goal may be to achieve *big* things in your life.

Do you think an *ant* would tell an *elephant* to take baby steps to succeed? Of course, not. So, why would you want to listen to the small thinkers tell you how to measure your own success? The people who *think small* want you to think small too. Their ultimate goal is to talk you out of taking bigger action steps. They know bigger steps will place you closer to your dreams and goals. Remove the unnecessary people, places, and things out of your life because they will slow you down. When it comes to your personal life, you must keep moving toward what *you* want to achieve, and not toward what *others* want you to achieve. You will succeed faster, when you begin to measure your success with your personal success ruler.

USE YOUR TOOLS TO BUILD YOUR SUCCESS

We have heard the saying, "When one door closes, another opens." New doors will open; however, we are living in a new era, which means *waiting* for the doors to open for us is past tense. Instead of "waiting" for doors to open for us, the time has arrived for us to start building our own doors to succeed.

It's one thing to *wait* for someone to come and repair your doorbell when it's broken. But, what if it's not your doorbell that's broken? When it comes to your life, progress, and success you must custom design and build your own door to succeed. You already have the tools *within* you to succeed. Now, it's time for you to *use* the tools within you to succeed.

Successful people build their own success. Oprah Winfrey, Bill Gates, and Donald Trump all built their own success. Yes, they have a creative team of people that helped them succeed. But, they are the visionary leader of their own teams. People enter into our lives to help and show us how to use our personal tools. Once someone has shown you how to use your *own* tools, implement what you learned. Always remember, nobody *can* or *will* build your success for you. You will need to start building your own success with your *own* tools.

What's inside your toolbox? Every tool you will need to succeed is already *within* you. Within you is a toolbox filled with the necessary tools you need to build and repair any and every aspect in your life. For example, your *mind* is your creative tool. Your *enthusiasm* is your energy tool. Your *action* is your performance tool. In other words, you hold all the tools that will enable you to "build" your own success.

As a progress thinker, you are fully equipped with your own unique tools. Don't let your tools sit around and rust. Start utilizing them. Once you start using your personal tools, you will be amazed at what you can and will build. What will you build today? Start building your own success and future with your own tools. The more you use your talents and strengths, the more doors will begin to open for you.

CLIMB YOUR OWN SUCCESS LADDER

There are a lot of success ladders throughout the world. Whose ladder are you climbing? Are you climbing someone else's ladder or are you climbing your own success ladder? As a progress thinker, start building and climbing your own success ladder.

As you climb your success ladder, you will encounter various challenges–good and bad–along the way to the top. For instance, one person will tell you, "Your dreams are impossible." Two people will laugh at your dreams. Three people will never talk to you again because they think you and your dreams are outlandish. If you're not careful, people will attempt to kick you off your own success ladder. Like I always say, "Don't give negative thinkers the satisfaction." You can't satisfy everybody, so why try? Despite the amount of people who laugh at you or try to pull you off your ladder–keep climbing until you reach the top.

While climbing your success ladder, there will be people who will walk out of your life. There will be people who will literally pressure you to make a choice between them or your dreams. For example, as the husband stated to his wife, "You said you loved me. Which one are you going to choose–me or your career?" As the wife stated to her husband, "If you love me, you would stay home with me and the kids. If you walk out that door I will leave you forever." Previous statements will do more than test your character, they will also see how determined you are to succeed.

Success is not easy when you have people pulling you *away* from what you want to achieve. That is why it's important to surround yourself with people who want you to succeed. Affiliate yourself with people who will "push you *toward*" achieving your goals. Eliminate the people who will "pull you *away* from" achieving your goals. Surround yourself with creative, successful, supportive, and positive-minded people.

As Vance Havner stated, "The vision must be followed by the venture. It is not enough to stare up the steps, we must step up the stairs." As progress thinkers, we are the masters of our own destiny. We are also the *builders* of our own success. As the builder of your own success ladder:

- *You* are the architect of your life's blueprint.
- *You* hold the master key to open doors in your life.
- *You* are the designated driver of your own life.
- *You* are the controller that is responsible for pressing your own start button.
- *You* are the producer of your own progress, results, and success.
- *You* are the executive producer of your own reality show and movie.

Whatever you want to achieve, you *can* achieve it. Remember, your success starts with *you*. Make your vision come to life with your actions. It will be your actions and results that will transform your dreams into reality. When your goal is to succeed, don't give up. Don't give up on what you want to achieve. Get focused and stay focused until you achieve your goals and dreams. In order to reach your pinnacle, you will need to keep moving *forward* and *upward* on your own success ladder.

SUCCESS IS ENDLESS

There are no limits to success. *Success is endless*. Success doesn't have an "One size fit all" policy attached to it. There are over a million ways to succeed, not just one way to succeed. No one ever said there's only one set of rules for success. In other words, there are no rules or laws that says, "Every person is prohibited from succeeding in more than *one* thing in his or her life." As a progress thinker, you can create your own rules to succeed. This is one of the benefits of being a progress thinker. You can succeed in as many endeavors as you want to succeed in.

FROM THE BOTTOM TO THE TOP

Do you know a successful person who started out broke, near broke, or worked at a dead end job? We all know someone who was either once financially broke or worked at a dead end job. When it comes to listing the successful people who started out broke, worked at dead end jobs, and/or started at the bottom of the success ladder the list is endless.

If you think that you're traveling on a dead end road, it's never too late to turn your life around. There are numerous successful people who turned their lives around. Many of them started at the bottom and worked their way up the success ladder. Speaking of ladders, even "the fiddler on the roof" had to start somewhere before reaching the top. If you notice, it's not where you *start*; it's where you're *going* that will make the difference.

Most people strive toward success not because they are looked upon as failures, but because they want a better view from their own success ladder. Whether you're afraid of heights or not, why would you want to stay on the *ground* level, when you can have the best view from the *penthouse* level?

As a progress thinker, you design your own success. There are various steps that you can take to design your own success. Here are two quick steps. First step, begin to look at your big picture. Mentally visualize what you want to achieve. Secondly, start taking action toward what you want to achieve. There are thousands of successful people who have climbed to the top of their own success ladder. You can do it too. You can start at the bottom of the ladder, and elevate yourself to the top of your own success mountain.

When you take the first step toward what you desire, you will be on your way to achieving it. When you believe in yourself, and constantly take action to achieve what you believe in, you will begin to build the ladder to your own success mountain.

CREATE YOUR OWN OPPORTUNITIES

A few years ago, a friend of mine named Andrew told me that one of his ultimate goals was to become a professional actor. As a new and aspiring actor, Drew didn't know many people in the movie industry.

When I first talked with Drew about his acting career, I inquired if he had ever thought about writing his own movie script. Without hesitation, Drew said, "No. The thought about writing a movie script never entered my mind." I suggested to him that he might want to consider writing his own movie script.

After telling Drew the profitable advantages of writing his own movie script, he started thinking more about the idea. While talking with Drew, I mentioned the importance of differentiating himself from the other new and professional actors and actresses. As I stated to Drew, "There are millions of people who want to be actors and actresses. Agents and movie producers hear that line every second of every day. What they want to see, hear, and have are people who are more creative." As Drew listened, I stated to him, "The key to your acting career will be your creativity. Start using your creativity. Once you begin to use your creativity, you will make yourself stand out from the millions of people who have the same dreams of acting as you."

As Drew's mental wheel started to turn, he said, "Wow! I never thought about that. What do you suggest that I do?" As Drew listened to my response, I said to him, "If you wrote your own movie script and produced it yourself that would allow you to star in your own movie." As the smile appeared on his face, I stated, "Writing your own script would give you more opportunities to create your own acting career. Most importantly, agents and movie producers would take you more serious as a person and actor." I paused for a moment to let the idea sink into his mind.

As Drew continued to look directly in my eyes, I said, "Look at Sylvester Stallone, he was once just like you. His dream was to become a professional actor. But, after being turned down countless times from acting auditions he did something different." Drew inquired, "What did he do differently?" I replied, "He used his creativity and wrote his own movie script, starring himself in the movie called *Rocky*."

A few weeks later, I saw Drew again; this time he had a gigantic smile on his face. He said, "Skip, I thought about what you said, and I've decided to write my own movie script." After hearing the great news, I congratulated Drew on his new progress toward becoming a successful actor.

A few months ago, I had the opportunity to attend an exclusive screening along with Drew's family and friends to see the first movie that he wrote, produced, and starred in. After watching his debut movie on the big theater screen, I didn't know if I should jump up and down, or start crying from joy. His movie and his acting skills were both creative and professional. The applause at the end of the movie displayed the successful outcome of Drew's movie. Although Drew stood up and thanked me in front of everyone, I would like to thank Drew for taking the initial action to launch his own acting career into stardom.

New opportunities present themselves to the people who are open-minded. Opportunities don't present themselves to the people who *wait* for them. Opportunities present themselves to the people who *create* them. At the beginning, Drew's mind was closed like a sealed vault to the idea of writing and producing his own movie. Why? Because the idea was brand new to him. Once Drew decided to open his mind to the new concept of writing his own movie, he instantly created a brand new opportunity for himself to build his own success mountain and become a successful actor.

As a progress thinker, you are fully equipped with the right tools to achieve what your heart desires. What will you build and achieve today? Imagine yourself achieving your dreams and goals. See yourself enjoying your forthcoming achievements and rewards.

WHERE ARE YOU LOCATED?

In most shopping malls, we usually see *location maps* near the entrance and in the middle of the mall that says, "You Are Here." As a progress thinker, when was the last time you asked yourself, "Where am I located in my life?"

Where are you now? Where would you like to go? What are you doing to get there? If "X" marked the spot of your *location* in life, where would you be? Would you be *at*, *near*, or *past* your destination? In order to reach your destination, you must know where you're currently located. Once you know where you're located, you will have a better understanding of where to go next.. If you never move toward your destination, you will keep yourself from reaching your destination. Why would you want to remain at the *same* location, when you can travel and see the whole world?

As the saying goes, "You have to start somewhere." It doesn't matter *where* you start, what matters the most is that you *do* start. There are numerous successful people who started out broke. In the book *Dare to Win*, Mark Victor Hansen, the co-author of *Chicken Soup for the Soul*, explained how he filed for bankruptcy before launching the mega *Chicken Soup for the Soul* book series. Though Mark Victor Hansen started out broke, he didn't remain broke. Today, the *Chicken Soup for the Soul* series of books has sold over 88 million copies.

There are millions of achievers who started out working at low paying and dead end jobs. In spite of their situation, they found a way to succeed. Did you know most of the people who are wealthy today, were once at the bottom of the success ladder?

Kenneth Cole, the famous designer of shoes, clothes, leather goods, and accessories once sold peanuts at Shea Stadium before he became a successful entrepreneur. Diane "Queen Latifah" Owens, the recording artist and actress, worked at a fast food restaurant before she became a celebrity. Dwayne "The Rock" Johnson, the professional wrestler turned actor, once had only $7 to his name before he became a millionaire. Anthony Robbins, the peak performance expert and author, described in his book *Awaken The Giant Within* how he once worked as a janitor. Tony, talked about how he went from working *inside* of a particular building, to *flying over the building* in his personal jet helicopter where he once worked. If you notice, dreams come true when you take action toward your dreams.

Action is mandatory for success. You might start out at the bottom, but you don't have to stay at the bottom. Your progress and success will start once you place yourself in the direction, in which you want to succeed. What is your ultimate goal? Are you moving toward your ultimate goal or away from it? The latter question is one that you need to ask yourself every day. The more you mentally and physically aim toward what you want to achieve, the more you will enhance your accuracy to hit the center (bull's-eye) of your target. You will succeed when you continuously take action toward your goals.

As a progress thinker, there will be several paths on your journey. Select the paths that will lead you to the next level. In his book *Put Your Dreams To The Test*, John C. Maxwell was correct when we wrote, "All dreams are outside our comfort zone. Leaving that zone is a price we must pay to achieve them." To reach the summit of your success mountain, you must be willing to keep stepping outside of your comfort zone. There will be challenges along the way, but don't let that stop you from achieving your goals. Keep climbing. Keep aiming higher. Keep looking forward and upward. Keep challenging yourself to get better every single day. Before you know it you will be on the golden path that will lead you to the top of your own success mountain.

14

MAXIMIZE YOUR NOW

"Victory is NOW!"
–MOTHER HICKS

Preparation is a necessity for success. When you want to succeed, you must *get ready* to succeed. If you don't *prepare* yourself for success, how do you think you will succeed? It's one thing to plan for tomorrow; however, it's important to make a game plan for you to *succeed* today.

It's been said, "Yesterday is history. Tomorrow is a mystery. And today? Today is a gift. That's why we call it the Present." Yesterday is gone forever, so place it behind you. Make *today* your focal point. Focus your mind, time, energy, and action on what you will achieve today.

The former Prime Minister of the United Kingdom, Margaret Thatcher, once stated, "Look at a day when you are supremely satisfied at the end. It's not a day when you lounge around doing nothing, it's when you've had everything to do and you've done it!" Make today and every day your best day. Reward yourself by maximizing TODAY!

FOCUS ON THE IMPORTANT TASKS

When I first started making the preparation to launch my own company, I met with a business advisor. After listening to my ideas, he simply asked me one question, "Which idea will be the most enjoyable and the most profitable one for you?"

As my mind quickly tried to search for an answer, the business advisor asserted, "For your company to succeed, you will need to focus on achieving your most important tasks." Being a new entrepreneur, I needed all the help that I could get, so receiving his professional advice really helped me think differently. It also encouraged me to set my priorities in order. From that day forward, I have been placing my focus on my most important tasks, which continues to help me produce more and faster results.

The author Stephen R. Covey said, "The key is not to prioritize what's on your schedule, but to schedule your priorities." You will accelerate your progress once you concentrate on achieving your *most* important tasks, rather than your *least* important tasks. What are your most important tasks? Do you have your priorities in order? If not, now is the perfect time for you to start setting your priorities. Knowing your priorities will do more than keep you focused on what you want to achieve, it will avoid you from wasting valuable time.

One effective way to achieve multiple tasks is by first writing down the tasks you want to accomplish. Then, review your list of tasks. As you review your list, select the most important tasks. Then prioritize each task by placing the most important tasks at the top of your list. After you have completely prioritized your list, place your actions, energy, and focal point on achieving your most important tasks, starting with the first task on your list.

WHAT DO YOU WANT?

It's been said, "Discipline is the bridge between goals and accomplishments." Progress thinkers discipline themselves by placing their focal point on accomplishing their goals, instead of what is *between* them and their goals.

All of us have our own individual goals that we want to achieve. I remember attending a seminar where one of the speakers said, "I went to college and became a doctor because that's what my *parents* wanted me to do." As the speaker continued, she stated, "I love helping people and that is one reason why I became a professional speaker." In conclusion she said, "The main reason I became a professional speaker was because that's what *I* really wanted to do." Who's sitting in your driver's seat? Are you the driver of your life or does someone else have control of the steering wheel and the direction of your life?

> "If you don't design your own life plan, chances are you'll fall into someone else's plan. And guess what they may have planned for you? Not much."
> –JIM ROHN

Jim Rohn was accurate when he said, "If you don't design your own life plan, chances are you'll fall into someone else's plan. And guess what they may have planned for you? Not much." How many people do you know who strive to please *others*, yet they forget about pleasing *themselves*? Every day there are countless people who constantly try to please their parents, family, friends, boss, and co-workers. However, the same people forget or fail to strive at all to please themselves.

Rather than trying to live someone else's dreams, strive to live your own dreams. What do you really want to do in your life? What goals and dreams would you like to achieve? Remember, *you* are the only person who can physically live and enjoy your own life. Write down what you want to achieve. Most importantly, start focusing your mind and actions on achieving what *you* want to achieve in your own life.

PROVE IT TO YOURSELF

Have you ever experienced a time in your life when you mentally told yourself, "I'll *show* them" or "I'll *prove* to them that I can do it?" Mostly everyone has said or thought something similar to the previous comments, at least once in his or her lifetime.

There was a time in my life when I tried to prove myself to others. If they didn't believe in my dreams, I would mentally say, "Watch me. I'll prove it." If someone told me that I couldn't succeed, I would say, "I'll show you." While going through my "I'll *prove* it" and "I'll *show* them" stage, I learned that the more I tried to *prove* myself to every person who told me that I couldn't succeed, the more I showed and proved to myself that I couldn't *please* or *prove* myself to everyone.

The comedian Bill Cosby said, "I don't know the key to success, but the key to failure is trying to please everybody." You can prove yourself to a few people, but you can't prove yourself to everyone. For example, if you try to prove yourself to everyone, you will make it difficult for yourself to live and enjoy your own life, because you will fall into the trap of trying to please everyone else, except yourself. Start asking yourself, "What will I accomplish by trying to please others?"

As the saying goes, "Action speaks louder than words," When you do your best, you won't have to prove yourself to others because your actions and results will speak for you. When you *improve* yourself, you will *prove* yourself. The more you *improve* yourself, the more your results will be displayed for others to see. When you want to *prove* something to someone, make sure you first *prove* it to yourself. One of the most effective ways that you can *prove* yourself to others is by first *proving it to yourself.*

As a progress thinker, prove to yourself that you can stand up on your own feet. Prove to yourself that you will go the extra mile to succeed, despite the obstacles in your way. Prove to yourself that you will go beyond what you achieved yesterday and last year. Prove to yourself that you are someone special. Prove to yourself that you have more to give, without giving up. Prove to yourself that you will do whatever it takes to become the best person that you can be.

IF IT'S WORTH IT…GO FOR IT!

A professional athlete once told me, "People would rather see, meet, and talk about celebrities, rather than put in the hard work to become a celebrity." He was speaking from his own experience. In his professional career, he received a lot of media exposure. In the midst of his stardom, fans sent him letters expressing their opinions about how much he *didn't deserve* to be a professional athlete. This is a person who put in the hard work and long hours for years to become one of the best in his profession.

As a professional, he usually started his training early in the morning, while most people were sleeping. He worked out hard at the gym and jogged miles to condition his body to get physically   strong. He made sacrifices in his personal and professional life. Even during his times of adversity, he did whatever it took to keep moving forward to achieve his ultimate goals. At the end, his hard work and long hours paid off for him to excel in his profession. In conclusion, he stated to me, "Every moment was worth it."

> *"Being on top in itself is not the reward, but the sheer pain, sweat and determination it took to get there."*
> –KRU PHIL NURSE

The Muay Thai champion Kru Phil Nurse once stated, "Being on top in itself is not the reward, but the sheer pain, sweat and determination it took to get there." It's easy for people to say, "You don't deserve it" when they don't know what you had to go through mentally, emotionally, physically, and financially to succeed.

When it comes to success, most people only notice the *end results*. In other words, they only "see" the *rewards at the end of success*. There are people who never think about or physically see what successful people have to literally go through "before" they reach success. They don't *see* the progress it takes for a person to become successful. They don't *see* the long hours of sweat, tears, hard work, commitment, and persistence that successful people must constantly go through *before* they literally succeed.

As I'm writing this chapter, it's 3:09 AM in the morning. Besides the students who are studying for their final exams and the people who can't sleep, how many people do you think are up and typing at 3 o'clock in the morning? If you notice, no one can see the long hours and the behind the scenes progress and persistence that I am putting into this book. However, at the end, my determination and hard work will payoff, and it will be well worth it. How do I know? Because you are reading the book. I am constantly burning the midnight oil, even in the daytime for my readers, clients, and audiences. I want to make sure that I provide innovative and effective resources that will transform and elevate you to the next level in your personal and professional life.

THE "STRONG WHY"

When you know "why" you are aiming toward your dreams and goals, you will become more focused with a definite purpose to achieve what you desire. When you have a "strong why" in your life, it will attach a strong determination for you to succeed.

A *strong why* is equivalent to having a *strong purpose*. For example, when you go to the fitness center do you workout just to say, "I workout" or do you workout to lose weight, tone your body, and keep your cardiovascular system operable, so you can look and feel good? The latter will give you a stronger purpose to physically work on your body. Many people don't like to workout or exercise because they look at it as a task. The people who enjoy working out don't view exercising as a task; they focus on how it will make them feel.

Every successful person has a "strong why" attached to his or her actions. The real pleasure comes when you know exactly *why* you're taking the action. When we have a *strong why* in front of us, we tend to work harder and more creatively. For instance, a single mother named Patty knew exactly *why* she woke up early each morning to start her day. Her *why* was to make sure that her daughter Nicole received the best education possible. As a single mother, Patty diligently worked two jobs so she could enroll her daughter in a private school.

Although Patty never went to college, she made personal sacrifices for Nicole to attend college. Day after day, year after year, Patty worked long hours to keep her daughter in the private school. The day arrived when Patty's daughter Nicole graduated from the private school, received a full scholarship, and went to college. Did Patty have a *strong why*? You bet she did.

Having a strong why will thrust upon you courage, creativity, commitment, and persistence. When your back is against the wall and you have a *strong why* in front of you, you will find or create a way to do whatever it takes to get your back off the wall to succeed.

When was the last time you gave yourself a *strong reason* to succeed in your life? Write down your personal goals and attach a "strong why" to them. Write down *why* you must achieve your goals. When you attach a *strong why* you must succeed, you will do more than take action steps, you will do whatever it takes to make it happen.

FAR OR NEAR REPORT

The majority of successful people have goals. Many of them have big goals. While some have small goals. Many of them have short, mid, and long-range goals. Most successful people have personal and professional goals. Having goals will help you achieve your dreams and ideas.

Setting goals is a vital element to every progress and success. Writing goals is one of the most effective ways that continue to help more people succeed. First, start writing down the goals you want to achieve. Secondly, attach a *strong why* you must achieve your goals. Next, *start taking physical action* toward the goals you want to achieve.

How often do you monitor your progress toward achieving your goals? It's one thing to say, "I have my goals." However, it's another thing when you know how *far* or *near* you are to accomplishing your goals. There is a scene in the animation movie called *Shrek 2*, where the Donkey, Shrek, and Fiona are on their way to Far Far Away to meet Fiona's parents. While on the road toward Far Far Away, Donkey continuously and impatiently asks, "Are we there yet?"

Though Donkey's inquiry, "Are we there yet?" took place within the animated movie, this is a question countless people ask themselves on a daily basis. Every day there are more people traveling and looking for their own golden brick road that will lead them to their destination called *success*. Although success is a reachable destination, there are some people who are traveling on their journey without a roadmap, GPS, or a game plan, as they constantly ask themselves over and over again, "Am I there yet?"

If you took a "success survey" you would discover that most people want to succeed and become successful in their lives. In the survey, you would also find that many people don't know how *far* or *near* they really are from their destination called *success*. Why? Because they never took the time to write down their goals, nor did they monitor their progress toward achieving their goals.

Do you know how *far* or *near* you are to achieving your goals? Having a *far* or *near report* will show you exactly how close you are to accomplishing your goals. As you take action to accomplish your goals, write down all the accomplishments you are making toward achieving your goals. There is an advantage to having your own *far* or *near report*. It will display your productive activities (what actions you are taking) and monitor the effective steps (what results you are producing) you are making toward achieving your goals.

Write down your goals on a piece of paper. Next, write down the action steps you are taking toward achieving your goals. Before you go to bed, review your achievements. Reviewing your *far* or *near* report daily will enable you to measure your progress toward accomplishing your goals.

CONGRATULATE YOURSELF

Have you ever performed a task so well that you felt as though someone should have thanked you or congratulated you for doing the task? If you said yes, what usually happens after you complete a task? If no one is around you, typically nothing happens. At times you will notice that many people will overlook the tasks you've successfully accomplished.

I would like to briefly talk about "waiting" in this chapter of the book. Many of us are constantly getting disappointed because we *wait* and depend on others to *thank* or *congratulate* us for a job well done. *Waiting* on someone to tell you, "Thank you" or "Great job" is like *waiting* on a cow to milk itself. *Waiting* will prolong your progress to succeed. When you *wait* or depend on someone to tell you "when" or "if" you've done a great job, you will always delay your own progress and success. Think about it. What if no one tells you, "great job" or "thank you" then what would you do? As a progress thinker, you don't have to *wait* for others to congratulate you to start enjoying your life. You can start enjoying your life by congratulating yourself daily.

> *"You don't have to wait for others to congratulate you to start enjoying your life. You can start enjoying your life by congratulating yourself daily."*

As I'm writing, I can't help but to think back to a few weeks ago, when I e-mailed one of my friends. As usual, I knew my e-mail would find her working diligently. So, instead of writing an extensive e-mail, I did something different. I simply sent her a brief e-mail with the words, "Congratulations!" as my subject.

Puzzled from my brief e-mail, she wanted to know where was the rest of my e-mail. She responded to my e-mail by saying, "What are you congratulating me for?" When I replied back to her, the following is what I said to her: "I want to take this moment to congratulate you for everything that you've accomplished in your life. As a single mother, I would like to congratulate you for being a loving, caring, and wonderful mother to your child. Congratulations for being a supportive friend. Congratulations for knowing who you are as a person and for literally going for what you want to achieve in your life. Also, if you haven't congratulated yourself lately, I wanted to remind you that you have plenty to congratulate yourself about every day."

As a progress thinker, there is always something you can congratulate yourself about. When you accomplish something, congratulate yourself.

Start congratulating yourself more, on a daily basis. The following are a few reasons you can *congratulate* yourself:

- Congratulate yourself for being a mother and/or father.
- Congratulate yourself for working out or losing weight.
- Congratulate yourself for being able to pay your monthly bills on time.
- Congratulate yourself for taking your kids to school and/or practice safely, and picking them up on time.
- Congratulate yourself for having a job, or having your own company, and making it to work on time.
- Congratulate yourself for completing tasks and meeting deadlines successfully.
- Congratulate yourself for overcoming the hardships and challenges in your life.
- Congratulate yourself for not giving up in your life.
- Congratulate yourself for going back to school to continue your education.
- Congratulate yourself for meeting and surrounding yourself with new and positive thinking friends.
- Congratulate yourself for reading *Think Progress*, so you can start making more progress in your life.
- Congratulate yourself for having an open-mind, so you can learn more and achieve new goals in your life.
- Most importantly, congratulate yourself for being *you*.

Did you congratulate yourself today? You are a unique person. As a unique person, start *congratulating* yourself in your own unique way. If you don't congratulate yourself on a daily basis nobody else will. When you do productive tasks, simply congratulate yourself for doing the tasks. Live your life knowing that you've done your best. When you achieve something, and you know deep within yourself that you've done a great job, simply tell yourself, "I did a great job." As a matter of fact, why not take it up a few notches? With a big smile on your face and with enthusiasm, proudly tell yourself, "I did an outstanding job!" The more you congratulate yourself, the more you will continue to advance your progress to new heights.

THE PERFECT MOMENT TO START...NOW!

Once upon a time, I didn't know anyone who could or would help me succeed. Nonetheless, the more risks I took, the more I continued to place myself outside of my comfort zone. This placed me in the realm to meet the right people who helped me change my life.

In my lifetime, I've had the opportunity to meet Fortune 500 executives, renowned professional speakers, doctors, judges and lawyers, movie stars, professional athletes, I've worked with all ages from youth to the elderly. I am not afraid to say, "Every person that I've met in my life has taught me something new and valuable about life."

As human beings, we *learn* by teaching each other. We learn from *others*, just like others learn from *us*. Dr. Robert H. Schuller's book *Tough Times Never Last, But Tough People Do!* was definitely an eye-opener for me. The title of the book seemed as though it was silently yelling my name. Before I read Dr. Schuller's book, I was going through hardships. While reading *Tough Times Never Last, But Tough People Do!* I learned how to stop looking <u>at</u> my adversity and learned to start looking <u>through</u> my adversity.

As Dr. Schuller stated in his book, "Take care? People who take care never go anywhere. Take a chance! Take charge! Take control!" And that's exactly what I did. For instance, instead of waiting for the renowned *one day, some day,* and *perfect day* to arrive, which neither "day" is an *official day* of the week, I challenged myself mentally, emotionally, and physically to make *every day* my best day.

As a progress thinker, you create your own perfect days and moments. Have you been looking for the *perfect moment*? If so, now is the *perfect moment* you've always been looking for in your life. Now is the perfect day and moment to start enjoying your life and maximizing your potential. Now is the perfect day and moment to start building your own success mountain. You can elevate yourself to the penthouse level of success once you start the process. Start with what you have *now*. If you don't *start* taking action to achieve your goals and enjoy your life *now*, when will you start? Why not start today? Take a chance! Take charge! Take control! The perfect moment has arrived...Start NOW!

MULTIPLY WHAT YOU HAVE

As I previously stated, when I first launched Skip Williams Communications, I didn't have a lot of money. As a matter of fact, I started my company when I was just a few dollars and cents away from being broke...literally.

Although I didn't have a lot of money, I learned a very important lesson in my life: In order to make progress in anything, you must *start* with what you have *right now*. This may sound a little farfetched to you. However, as a progress thinker, you must *start somewhere* to arrive at the destination that you are mentally and physically aiming toward in your life.

I prevailed personally and professionally because I learned how to work with the little bit that I had at the moment. Though I didn't have a lot to work with, I learned how to capitalize on what I had at that time in my life. I learned how to use and maximize the small amount of money that I had accessible. Plus, I used the few sources that I had available to me. Also, this was the era in my life when books became my best friend.

The books I read taught me how to advance my personal skills and knowledge. The more books I read, the more my mind thirsted for more. The more I learned, the more I applied it. Once I opened my mind to the new strategies that I learned, and implemented the strategies, my mind, skills, and results began to soar to new heights. Yes, I had obstacles in front of me, but I refused to allow the setbacks to stop me from achieving more in my life. I had BIG dreams, just like you. I wanted to physically achieve my goals and fulfill my dreams, just like you. I wanted to be successful, just like you. I wanted to change and improve my life, just like you. I wanted happiness, just like you. I wanted to not only "prove" myself to *others*, but also *prove something to myself*, just like you.

What steps did I take to succeed? First, I gave myself the permission to succeed. Secondly, I stopped waiting on my dreams to come to me, so I read self-help, autobiographies, business and investing books, which prepared me to launch my own company. Third, I physically wrote down my personal and professional goals, which enhanced passion to achieve them. Fourth, on the top of my list of "*excitements*" I wrote the words, "Aim High and Take Action NOW!" Fifth, I took unstoppable action toward my goals, until I achieved them.

The moral of my life story: You don't have to have a lot, at the beginning, to start living your dreams and enjoying your life. I started with the *little* things that I had available to me. Within the process of building my own success mountain, I became a more creative person. It was my determination and actions that enhanced my life to new levels. You can do the same. You may think you don't have a lot. However, you have more than enough to succeed. The key is to *start* where you are with what you have *right now* in your life. If you only have $100 in your pocket and/or bank account combined, you can start with what you have *right now*. Use your creativity and start looking for opportunities that will enable you to multiply what you currently have in your life.

INVEST IN YOURSELF

Are you an investor? If so, do you invest in stocks, bonds, mutual funds, or real estate? Are you happy with your investments? Now, let me ask you: "What do you know about the companies that you are *investing* your money into?"

Research studies have shown that some investors usually invest their money with limited knowledge on their investments. There are some investors who hand their money over to a broker and say, "Here...invest it." Out of all the things you have invested in, when was the last time you *invested* in yourself? Let's go a step further. What do you know about yourself? You should know more about yourself, than about the companies that you invest your money into. Investing in oneself is a smart investment. Start asking yourself, "How can I *invest* in myself?" Once you start investing in yourself, it will be one of the best investments you will ever make in your life.

A few years ago, I read an interesting story about Robert Johnson, the founder of BET, which is also known as Black Entertainment Television. In the midst of launching BET off the ground, a person whom Mr. Johnson knew decided to invest in the company. The investment allowed Mr. Johnson to stay in control of BET (which he has since sold to Viacom). One day out of the blue, Mr. Johnson asked the investor, "Why did you do the deal where I (Mr. Johnson) ended up controlling the majority of the company?" The investor told Mr. Johnson, "I always knew you would *work harder for yourself*, than you would for me."

As progress thinkers, we grow when we invest in ourselves. You will begin to achieve more, once you stop telling yourself, "I'm *not* worth it" or "I'm *not* smart enough." You are smart enough, creative enough, and worth it enough to *invest* in yourself. Regardless of who or how many people "invest" in you, your ideas, and/or your company, remember you are always the majority investor in yourself.

Self-investment is a requirement for success. You will need to invest in yourself to succeed. Every investment doesn't pertain to stocks, bonds, mutual funds, CD's, or real estate. For example, the way you *think about yourself* is a self-investment; think optimistic. Your *self-confidence* is a valuable self-investment; believe in yourself. Your *wardrobe* is a self-investment; buy and wear the best clothes that will present you well. *The people you surround yourself with* are investments. Affiliate yourself with the right people who will help you improve and advance your personal and professional life.

Investing in yourself will reward you abundantly. Begin to look at everything you do, as a *self-investment*. Start thinking like wealthy investors by asking yourself, "Is this a *good* or *bad* investment for me?" Use your mind, time, energy, action, and money in a profitable manner. The more you *invest* in yourself, the more you will continually build profitable assets that will double and triple your *self*-ROI (return on investment).

PUT GREEN LIGHTS ON YOUR PATH

While unsuccessful people are complaining about the amount of steps that are required to succeed; successful people are going beyond the complaining stage, and taking the required steps to succeed.

When Bill Gates and Paul Allen started *Microsoft* they didn't complain about all the work that needed to be done. They simply put in the hours of work that was needed for them to produce their innovative software. The two creative entrepreneurs' hard work, mental focus, physical action, and persistence paid off tremendously. The more action they took toward their goals, the more green lights appeared on their path.

Bill Gates and Paul Allen took the mandatory steps to succeed. They aimed high, took action, and physically, as well as financially, succeeded. You can do the same. You don't have to be a billionaire or have a million dollars in your bank account to start living and enjoying your life. You can *start* with what you have in your life right now.

It's usually the *red lights* that stop most people from succeeding. To succeed, you must remove the red lights out of your mind, and replace them with *green lights*. In other words, replace your *old* "I can't" thoughts with brand *new* "I can" thoughts. You *can* succeed once you stop telling yourself that you *can't* succeed. Don't stop yourself from succeeding. Start doing whatever it takes to succeed. When you aim high and take action toward what you're aiming to achieve, you will not only accelerate your progress, you will begin to place more green lights on your path to succeed.

UNLEASH YOUR POTENTIAL

Andrew Jackson, the 7th President of the United States, once stated, "Take time to deliberate, but when the time for action arrives, stop thinking and go in." How long have you been thinking about your dreams and goals? When was the last time you took action toward your dreams and goals? Take this moment to tell yourself, "I have too much potential to waste it."

You've been *thinking* about your goals and dreams. You've *thought* about them. Now, *do something* to achieve your goals and dreams. Don't limit or waste your potential. Unleash and maximize your potential. The moment you unleash and maximize your potential, you will begin to advance your life, progress, and success. If you're currently being challenged, what are you doing to overcome your challenges? How many more days must pass by before you decide to improve or change your results? How long are you going to continue to sit and talk about what you would like to achieve in your life? When are you going to literally stand up and take action toward what you want to achieve? The longer you refrain from taking action, the longer you will delay your progress and success.

> *"Take time to deliberate, but when the time for action arrives,*
> *stop thinking and go in."*
> –ANDREW JACKSON

New opportunities are waiting on you. But, they are not going to automatically come to you. The time has arrived for you to open your mind and take action, so that you can meet new people, go to new places, and achieve new goals.

In his book *Make Today Count* John C. Maxwell stated, "Every day I will focus on my financial game plan so that each day I will have more, not fewer options." Every day, from the moment you wake, you have the option to either aim higher or aim lower. You have the option to think bigger or think smaller. You have the option to get up and take action or stay in the bed. As a progress thinker, every action you take or refuse to take will exemplify the level of your progress, results, and success. It doesn't matter if you're competing against a thousand people, a small team of people, or simply competing against yourself...you can succeed when you take action. Make today count. Unleash your potential and take action today.

TURN YOUR TALKING INTO ACTION

The poet and lecturer Ralph Waldo Emerson observed, "What you do speaks so loudly that I cannot hear what you say." Simply put, Talk is Cheap; Action is Priceless! It's not how loud you *think* and *talk* that will make the difference. It's how loud your *actions* and *results* are that will make the difference.

One of the most effective ways to express yourself is to let your *actions* speak for you. You don't have to talk a lot when you let your actions and results do all the talking for you. This also means you won't have to try to impress Carol, Bob, and Jim by telling them what you want to achieve in your life. There is no need to brag or boast about what you want to achieve. Why? Because once you begin to take action and achieve your dreams and goals–your actions, results, and achievements will brag and boast for you. In other words, when you achieve your goals and dreams, people will see your accomplishments. If you notice, it's not what you *say*, it's what you *do* that will produce your results.

Action is a mandatory requirement for every achievement. I have heard people use the phrase, "Your word is your bond." However, they never mention "action" and "results" in the same sentence. It's our actions and results that ultimately make our "word" become our bond. It will be your actions and results that will make your "words" come to fruition.

> *"You can't build a reputation on what you are going to do."*
> –HENRY FORD

Henry Ford, the founder of the Ford Motor Company, once said, "You can't build a reputation on what you are going to do." As a progress thinker, it's time to turn your thinking and talking into *action* and *results*. As some people like to say, "Put your *money* where your mouth is." To paraphrase it, "Put your *action* and *results* where your mouth is." Keep in mind, nothing happens without action and results. High achievers take action to succeed. Under achievers complain about the action they must take to succeed.

One valuable lesson I learned in my life, and I still use this principle: Don't *tell* everyone what you want to achieve. Refrain from telling others what you're going to do. Instead of telling them, simply go out and achieve it. It's one thing to say what you want to do. It's another thing, when you physically step out and do it. Talking about what you want to achieve will keep you at the starting line. When you take action toward what you want to achieve you will place yourself across the achievement line.

WHAT ELSE ARE YOU DOING?

What usually takes place when two people meet for the first time? After introducing themselves with their name and small talk, the next phrase that typically exits someone's mouth is the renowned question, "What *do* you do?"

There is nothing wrong with asking people what they do for a living. But, let me ask you a question: Do you think people literally ask Oprah Winfrey, Bill Gates, Will Smith, Julia Roberts, Tom Cruise, Steven Spielberg, Madonna, Beyoncé Knowles, Tiger Woods, and Donald Trump the question, "What *do* you do?"

When you maximize your potential and constantly strive toward excellence, people shouldn't have to inquire about what you *do* for a living. Instead of someone asking you, "What *do* you do?" They should be asking you, "What *else* are you doing?"

15

CHAMPION RESULTS

"Success doesn't know the meaning of giving up.
The people who succeed never give up on their journey.
They just become more creative to achieve
their ultimate goals."
–SKIP J. WILLIAMS

Let's take a mental stroll inside the supermarket. As you and I stroll down the aisle with our shopping carts you notice two different washing detergents sitting side-by-side on the shelf. One washing detergent is your *favorite* brand, and the other detergent is a *generic* brand. On the front of the *generic* brand box in big, bright, and bold letters it says, "NEW" and "IMPROVED." If you had to choose <u>one</u> of the two detergents, which detergent would you buy? Would you purchase your favorite detergent? Or, would you buy the "NEW" and "IMPROVED" *generic* detergent?

When a shopping survey was conducted, the majority of shoppers stated they would buy the "NEW" and "IMPROVED" washing detergent. Though it wasn't their favorite brand, they wanted something *new* and *improved*. When was the last time you did something "NEW" to *improve* your life?

WHAT IT TAKES TO SUCCEED?

One afternoon, while in the midst of a Q&A (Question & Answer), someone in the audience asked me, "What are the requirements to become successful?" After hearing the question, I could have given an extensive list of requirements for success. However, I chose to keep the list concise by simply stating one word, "Improvement." *Improvement* is the core necessity to become successful. Every thought that enters your mind, every action you take, as well as every result you produce could use some *improvement*.

The more you improve yourself, the more you will continue to elevate the height of your success. Improvement has transformed average people into extraordinary people. There are individuals and teams that went from last place to first place, simply because they worked on improving themselves. They improved themselves, as individuals. Also, they improved the quality of their performance as a team. It's improvement that creates champions.

Your personal effectiveness starts with your personal improvement. When you want to produce effective results, you will need to start with *self-improvement*. Improving yourself, on a daily basis, will improve your results daily. Whatever you achieved yesterday, you can *improve* it today. Improvement will make you stronger, healthier, wealthier, and better. Improvement will make you the best. Winners are always striving to improve themselves, their performance, and their results. You don't have to be an athlete to become a champion. However, you must be willing to *improve* yourself every single day to become a champion.

One advantage to improvement is that it's never too late to start improving yourself. You can start improving yourself right now. There is always room for self-improvement. When it comes to self-improvement, it's endless. There is infinite space available for you to improve yourself in every area of your life spiritually, mentally, emotionally, physically, professionally, and financially.

Jim Rohn's mentor, Mr. Shoaff, once told him an empowering message that changed his life. Mr. Shoaff stated, "Work harder on yourself than you do on your job. If you work on your job, you can make a living. If you work on yourself, you can make a fortune." The power behind that message is like hitting a grand slam home run to win the World Series.

Take a moment and ask yourself, "How can I *improve* myself today?" Get in the habit of improving yourself. Focus on developing "new" and "improved" results. The more you improve yourself, the more you will enhance your self-worth. Start viewing yourself as a valuable asset. Every day look for innovative ways to add more value to yourself, your family and friends, your team, your company, and the people around you.

DARE TO MAXIMIZE

To succeed in anything, you must *start* somewhere. You are presently standing at the starting line that will change your life. Why wait until *tomorrow* to change your life, when *today* is already present?

The most influential eight words that changed my life came from Helen Keller when she said, "Life is either a daring adventure or nothing." Nothing will get accomplished sitting around doing nothing. For example, *doing nothing* comes from not challenging oneself. *Not challenging oneself* comes from not taking risks. *Not taking risks* comes from lack of "daring" oneself. When was the last time you "dared" yourself to take a risk?

In life, we all need to *dare* ourselves, at least once, to take a risk. When you *don't* want to do something that is the best time to *dare* yourself to take a risk. If your life isn't exciting and adventurous, you're not taking enough risks. When you take more risks, you will place more "excitement" into your life. Don't minimize your risks; MAXIMIZE your risks. Become a risk taker. Do something new and different today. Take a risk that will place you closer to your dreams and goals.

CHAMPIONS ARE RISK TAKERS

The renowned psychologist, advice columnist, and author Dr. Joyce Brothers, once stated, "Accept that all of us can be hurt, that all of us can and surely will at times fail. I think we should follow a simple rule: If we can take the worst, take the risk." When was the last time you took a *risk*? When it comes to taking risks, you can either take the risks, or wait for life to make you take the risks.

The word "waiting" to a risk taker is like telling him or her that something is impossible. Risk takers don't believe in the word *impossible*. Nor do risk takers believe in *waiting* on someone or something special to appear into their personal arena to cheer for them. A risk taker's cheers come from his or her own actions, results, and achievements. The more risks they take, the louder the cheers.

> *"Accept that all of us can be hurt, that all of us can and surely will at times fail. I think we should follow a simple rule: If we can take the worst, take the risk."*
> –DR. JOYCE BROTHERS

In the words of the poet T.S. Eliot, "Only those who will risk going too far can possibly find out how far one can go." Risk takers are always pushing their envelopes beyond the limits. I concur. This is one of the main reasons why I started my own company, because I get the opportunity to push my own envelope every day. I would rather push my own envelope, rather than wait for someone else to hand me an envelope with a pink slip inside of it notifying me that my services are no longer needed.

Who's holding your envelope? Are *you* or someone else holding your envelope? Are you *pushing or pulling* your envelope? If you're pushing, how far have you pushed your envelope thus far in your life? How far are you willing to push your envelope, so you can reach the next level?

A risk taker is someone who is <u>not</u> afraid to take risks. It's the risk takers who accumulate the most success in the world. Why? Because they take more risks to succeed. Instead of postponing or putting their goals and dreams on the back burner, risk takers place their goals and dreams in front of them, and charge at them full steam. In other words, they physically go out and make their own success happen.

My first major introduction to taking risks occurred when I was in the U.S. Marine Corps (USMC). During boot camp, our drill instructors constantly challenged us to take risks. Every moment of the day, we were perpetually challenged to take more risks, even when we didn't feel like it. The risks that I took in the USMC helped me become who I am today. Every day I push myself to take more calculated risks, as I constantly challenge myself to achieve more.

Risk takers know there is always more to achieve. I like the way John Sculley defined risk takers. He said, "People who take risks are the people you'll lose against." In other words, it's the risk takers who become champions. For example, entrepreneurs take risks by launching their own companies. Leaders take risks by leading others. Risk takers know the more risks they take, the more they will increase their opportunities to prosper.

As a progress thinker, what *risks* will you take to prosper? You have the qualities of a champion. Start taking risks like a champion. Once you start taking risks, you will begin to standout like a champion.

UNLEASH YOUR RISK TAKER

The biologist Thomas Henry Huxley used the following words for his perception of taking risks, "Perhaps the most valuable result of all education is the ability to make yourself do the thing you have to do, when it ought to be done, whether you like it or not."

Every success requires some form of risk taking. When we unleash our personal risk taker, we design our own future. If you have been holding yourself back from taking risks, now is the best time to unleash your risk taker.

Progress thinkers succeed because they take risks. For example, Madonna, the recording artist, took countless risks that led her to become a celebrity. She took a risk when she arrived in New York with less than $40 dollars in her pocket. Some people called her crazy for doing such a thing; nevertheless, Madonna believed in herself and took the risk anyway. The risks that Madonna took elevated her from a no-name person into a household name celebrity. Madonna wanted to achieve more in her life, so she took the necessary risks that enabled her to succeed.

Unleash your risk taker. If you're not taking risks, start taking a *few* risks. If you are taking risks, start taking *more* risks. What *risks* will you take to succeed? When you take the risks to succeed, you will create your own success.

IT'S WORTH THE RISK

We are all risk takers in one form or another. Some of us take more risks than others. Everything we do in life pertains to taking risks. Life itself is a risk. In life, there are various forms of taking risks. For example, we take risks every time we enter or exit our homes because we never know what may happen in the process. Millions of people take risks every time they play the lottery. They never know if their numbers will hit the jackpot or not. Whenever we call someone on the telephone we take a risk, because we never know if the person will answer the telephone, especially since the invention of Caller ID. Nonetheless, we take the risk and call the person anyway. If you noticed, taking risks are a part of life.

You can start taking risks with what you currently have in your life. It's not about *what you have* in your life that matters. What matters is *what you do with what you have*. When you start with what you currently have, you will eventually gain more of what you *want* and *need* along the way.

Progress thinkers are not afraid to take calculated risks. To succeed in anything, you must be willing to take a few risks. There is nothing wrong with taking risks. Become a risk taker. Learn a new language, travel to a new country, meet and surround yourself with new people, set and achieve new goals.

THE PREPARATION OF CHAMPIONS

I like the ingredients that the author William A. Ward used to define success: "Recipe for Success: *Study* while others are sleeping; *work* while others are loafing; *prepare* while others are playing; and *dream* while others are wishing." What are you doing to prepare yourself for your forthcoming success? Are you *wishing* or are you *preparing* for success?

Your success will depend on your preparation, game plan, actions, and results. To succeed, you must *prepare* yourself for success. Champions know in order for them to be victorious, they must continuously prepare themselves by practicing, studying, and putting forth their best effort. Are you putting forth your *best* effort or are you half-stepping and only putting forth a *little* effort?

Progress thinkers become champions because they push themselves to succeed. Champions are willing to do whatever it takes to go beyond the average. For example, when the average person gets tired and quits, champions catch their second wind and keep going. When the average person strives for an inch, champions challenge themselves to go the extra mile. When the average person says, "I *can't* go on", champions say, "I *will* go on."

Champions work hard because they know when they are sleeping there are thousands of people who are awake and working harder to become a champion too. For instance, there are champion bodybuilders who have won awards for the sculpture of their physique. The champion bodybuilder knows there are other bodybuilders who are striving to take his or her position as the champion. While the champion bodybuilder is snoozing, there are thousands of amateurs and professional bodybuilders working harder on their bodies. They are staying in the gym longer hours and lifting more weights, so they can prepare themselves to become the champion.

You may not be striving to become a professional bodybuilder, but you're striving for something. You are striving to achieve your goals and dreams. You are striving to keep food on the table, clothes on your back, and a roof over your head for yourself and your family.

Champions focus on producing effective results that will maximize their performance. As a progress thinker, you have champion qualities. Now, the key is to improve and maximize your qualities. People have asked me, "Skip, how can I become a champion?" My answer, "To become the best, you must do your best daily."

Every day work on improving your communication and people skills; so when you talk with others you will be prepared to hold an enjoyable conversation. Every day read 30-60 minutes on a subject in your profession. Every day challenge yourself to surpass what you accomplished yesterday, last week, and last year. Every day work on giving your best performance and producing your best results. Every day work on preparing yourself for what you are striving to achieve. When you keep preparing yourself and continue to put forth your best effort mentally, emotionally, and physically you will begin to produce champion results.

CHAMPIONS ARE SURVIVORS OF DEFEAT

When you don't succeed *the first* time around that doesn't make you a failure. It's only an indication that you need to adjust your success plan. A little adjustment can make a big difference in your results.

Progress thinkers are constantly modifying their success plan. They revise their plan, until they discover the right pieces to their success puzzle. Every successful person has experienced a taste of *defeat*. Defeat is not a good taste, and this is one reason why champions push themselves, because they don't want to taste it again.

It's the temporary defeats that build stronger achievers. Commence to look at your defeats as your *strength-builders*. It will be your temporary defeats that will build the strength to your character. It will be your temporary defeats that will lead you in the direction to become a stronger, more creative, and better person. Some people *fail* once or ten times; however, Thomas Edison encountered what some people define as "failure" over a thousand times. Did Thomas Edison give up? No, he continued until he succeeded. Champions keep moving forward despite their setbacks and obstacles.

The martial artist and actor Bruce Lee once said, "Defeat is not defeat unless accepted as reality in your own mind." I've definitely had my encounter with defeat on more than a few occasions. There were ventures that I attempted in my life that failed. However, within *every* attempt, I learned something new that taught me how to succeed. Through my personal setbacks, I've learned to look at life differently. For instance, in my mind, I believe that I've never been *defeated*, nor have I ever *failed* in my life. You may be asking how is that possible? Every *success* and *failure* starts in the mind. In my mind, I never *failed*, simply because I never let my mind accept failure. I conditioned my mind for "success," not failure.

> *"Defeat is not defeat unless accepted*
> *as reality in your own mind."*
> –BRUCE LEE

As a progress thinker, start viewing your defeats as temporary. When a temporary defeat arrives, keep in mind that you can conquer your defeats. To overcome your temporary defeats, your *beliefs* must be stronger than your *doubts*. Instead of doubting yourself, start believing in yourself. The more you believe in yourself, the stronger you will become as a person. The stronger you become as an individual, the stronger you will develop your bridge to overcome the *temporary defeats*.

THE WAKE-UP CALL OF DEFEAT

There are times when *defeat* is needed for us to grow. Defeat has its own unique way of strengthening us mentally, physically, spiritually, emotionally, and financially.

Temporary defeats are your personal wake-up calls. For example, when you experience a temporary defeat it will instantly make you pay closer attention to the results that you are producing. Temporary defeat doesn't mean *permanent* defeat. One way to succeed is to learn from your defeats. Never think of yourself as being *permanently* defeated, only *temporarily* defeated. For instance, if you attempt to accomplish one of your goals, and you don't succeed the first time around that is not a reason to quit. Don't quit on your dreams and goals. Keep pushing onward until you achieve your dreams and goals.

A *temporary defeat* is like a pit stop, which means you are positioned in a certain area only for a brief moment. If you're presently being challenged by a temporary defeat, remember, it's not permanent; it's only a *temporary* pit stop on your journey.

THE NEXT STEP UP THE LADDER

As you begin your journey up your success ladder, many people will forget to tell you "the first step" on your success ladder may be failure. If that happens, congratulations! That is an indication that you're on your way up the success ladder.

The novelist F. Scott Fitzgerald once stated, "Never confuse defeat with a final defeat." The majority of successful people have experienced some form of *temporary* failure or defeat on their success ladder. If you have experienced a minor defeat or failure on the first step of your success ladder, the only place you can go now is upward.

> *"Never confuse a single defeat with a final defeat."*
> –F. SCOTT FITZGERALD

As M.H. Alderson observed, "If at first you don't succeed, you are running about average." If you fail on the first step that you take, don't be afraid to take another step on your success ladder. Use your temporary failures and defeats as your stepping-stones. To succeed in anything, you must continuously take forward and upward steps on your success ladder, until you reach the top.

It doesn't matter how many times you try something and fail. What matters the most is how many times you get back on your success ladder.

For example, it took Colonel Sanders countless attempts before his *Kentucky Fried Chicken* special recipe became successful. There are people who succeeded on their twentieth attempt after failing nineteen times out of the twenty times. Refusing to give up, they finally succeeded on their twentieth attempt. Though it took twenty attempts to succeed, the twentieth try made up for *all* the other failed attempts.

Failing doesn't make you a failure. You're not a failure when you learn from your mistakes. Progress thinkers keep pressing onward despite the odds against them. To succeed, you must be willing to learn from your mistakes and failures. If you didn't achieve something the first time around, you're not a failure. Simply write down what *did* work, and what *didn't* work for you. Find and fix the flaws in your plan. Once you discover and fix your flaws, make another attempt toward what you want to achieve. It will be your *temporary* defeats that will teach you how to become more creative.

Success rewards the winners who refuse to quit. When you refuse to quit, you will triple your opportunities to succeed. This is why it's imperative that you keep tweaking your flaws and keep moving forward, because each tweak and step you take will place you closer to achieving your dreams and goals.

CHAMPIONS REFUSE TO SURRENDER

As Muhammad Ali, the boxing legend, once said, "Champions aren't made in gyms. Champions are made from something they have deep inside them: A desire, a dream and a vision. They have to have last-minute stamina, they have to be a little faster, they have to have the skill and the will. But, the will must be stronger than the skill." How strong is your personal *will* and *skills*?

Every person has a *will* and a *skill* to succeed in his or her life. It doesn't matter where you start; it matters where you finish. It doesn't matter how many times you have attempted something and it didn't work. What matters the most is that you keep attempting it, until you succeed.

Did you know "giving up" is the easiest thing to do in life? Think about it. To give up, all someone has to do is simply say the words, "I quit" or "I give up." Once a person decides to quit or give up that's it...GAME OVER. No happiness. No success. No rewards.

What usually happens after someone says, "I quit" or "I give up?" Everything just stops. The person's *mind* stops thinking. His or her *actions* stop moving. Their *results* quickly diminish. Giving up and quitting doesn't produce rewards and happiness. Giving up has a tendency to cause heartaches, sadness and a ton of pain and regrets.

Anybody can give up and quit. Champions refuse to give up or quit. No one remembers and applauds the people who gave up. People remember and applaud for those who *refuse to give up*. If you're contemplating on giving up, reject the thought out of your mind. Don't give up. Stand up! Why would you want to give up when you have the potential to accomplish more? When adversity appears on your journey, and whenever the thought of giving up enters your mind, tell yourself, "I can succeed. I must keep moving forward to succeed."

DON'T STOP YOUR LIFE. START YOUR LIFE.

A few years ago, I was asked to speak to a group of adults who were financially challenged. After I gave my speech, I asked the audience if they had any questions. Many of the attendees at the event raised their hands. Then, they commenced to ask me various questions, which I answered.

I can still remember the last question from the event. It came from a young lady sitting on the front row. She said, "Mr. Williams, have you ever thought about *giving up* on life?" The entire room was already silent. But, after she asked me that question, it seemed as though the entire room became *super* silent. So silent you could have heard a pin drop on the carpet. It was definitely a breathtaking moment.

Before I answered the question, I calmly walked closer toward the young lady. I stopped a few feet from her. As I stood right in front of her, looking directly into her eyes, I said to her, "I have never thought about giving up *in* or *on* my life. Neither should you. I know deep down inside of me, I have more to give in my life. You too, have more to give in your life." While standing in front of her, I concluded by saying, "Don't *stop* your life. *Start* your life."

If you are contemplating about giving up *in* or *on* your life, take a moment to ask yourself, "Why would I want to *give up*, when I have more inside of me to *give*?" The following are "*self-defeating*" words that will keep you from succeeding:

- "I give up"
- "I quit"
- "I can't"
- "I won't"
- "I'll never"

Giving up is <u>not</u> the answer to your problems. There is nothing great or rewarding about giving up. When you encounter challenges and hardships in your life, don't *give* up...GET UP!

As a progress thinker, keep moving forward. Don't stop your life. Start living and enjoying your life. There are an abundance of rewards ahead with your name on them. If you *give up*, how will you be able to receive your forthcoming rewards? Most importantly, you are a champion, and champions don't quit. You have the qualities of a champion. Start using your champion attributes.

GOALS WRITE THEIR OWN UNIQUE STORIES

There are a variety of names that are used to describe the word "goals." In business, *goals* are called a *business plan*. In sports, *goals* are called a *game plan*. Some people call their *goals,* a *to-do list.* Then, you have a handful of people who just scribble down a few words on the first piece of paper they see in their reach.

Joanne Kathleen Rowling, also known as J.K. Rowling, had a goal to write a book. Her book wasn't looked upon as your average book. J.K. Rowling's book was so innovative and unique that when she first submitted her book to an agent, the agent returned the book, refusing to represent her and her unparalleled book.

When J.K. Rowling found an agent that would represent her and her spellbound book, she encountered another challenge, which entailed 12 publishers rejecting her book. Although several publishers rejected her manuscript, J.K. Rowling's determination became one of her goals. She was determined to get her manuscript published. Finally, her determination paid off when a publisher accepted and gave her *Harry Potter* book the green light to be published. After the first *Harry Potter* book was released it became a bestseller.

Today, over 350 million copies of the *Harry Potter* series have sold and are still selling. The *Harry Potter* books have been produced into several movies, which has grossed over $2 billion dollars. Also, the success of the *Harry Potter* books has extended into numerous endorsement deals, which continues to gross millions of dollars. There is also a theme park ride called *The Wizarding World of Harry Potter* at Universal Orlando Resort.

J.K. Rowling went from living on social security to living her dreams. She went from a dreamer, to a goal setter, to a published author, to a very wealthy and successful bestselling author. As a progress thinker, is it time for you to write a new chapter in your life? If so, start by writing new goals for yourself to achieve.

GET EXCITED ABOUT YOUR GOALS

It's been said, "Winners make goals; losers make excuses." Having goals can make a difference in your progress, results, and success. Do you have goals? If so, have you written them down? If not, take a moment to write down your goals. After you have written down your goals, commit yourself to the goals you want to achieve. Most importantly, get *excited* about achieving your goals. When you get excited about your goals, and start taking action toward them, you will eventually transform your goals into fruition.

One of the most effective ways to succeed is to custom-design your own success. For example, instead of calling your goals the typical word, "goals." What if you started calling them, "EXCITEMENTS?" Think about it. You first have to get excited about your goals to achieve them. So, instead of prolonging the process, simply start calling your *goals* – "EXCITEMENTS" from the beginning.

16

PERSISTENCE BREEDS SUCCESS

"The difference between a successful person and others is not a lack of strength, not a lack of knowledge, but rather a lack of will."
–VINCE LOMBARDI

"We are down by three and the game is almost over. What do we do coach?" said one player. As the coach looked around at the players, he enthusiastically stated, "The game isn't over, *persistence* will get us through." Challenges will appear on your journey, but that's not a reason to give up. It will be your determination and persistence that will get you through.

What does a *house on the hill* and *success* have in common? Both are reachable. When it comes to success, there is one factor many people have a tendency to overlook…Success is attainable. The secret is out of the bag: YOU CAN SUCCEED!

Progress thinkers are known for constantly doing the things that others refuse to do. Many successful people don't enjoy everything that they do; nonetheless, they do the tasks anyway because they know completing the tasks will enable them to prosper.

No one ever said, "Success will be an easy task." Despite the amount of obstacles, adversities, setbacks and tasks that you have to go through to succeed, keep moving forward until you succeed. It's what you *do* in the midst of your progress that will define your success. For example, there will be some days when you will need to get up earlier than usual, so you can get a head start to complete your tasks on time. There will be moments when you will need to make more phone calls than you are used to making. There will be times when you will need to do things, when you really don't want to do them. Once you complete the tasks, it will be worth it.

Persistence is the secret to every success. When your objective is to be victorious, the game is never over. Why? Persistence breeds success. Winners never give up, due to their persistence to win. You will win, when you become persistent. Keep moving forward. Your unstoppable persistence will lead you to endless success.

PERSISTENCE WILL MOVE YOU FORWARD

At the moment, you may be traveling on some rough terrain in your life. For instance, the things you want to achieve may not be happening fast enough. The people you want *in* your life may have *exited out* of your life. When it seems as though things are not going right, remind yourself that it's all a part of the process that will enable you to succeed.

Have you ever seen a successful person and then asked yourself, "How did that person succeed?" It's simple. They took the essential steps toward what they wanted to achieve and they refused to stop, until they succeeded. That is called *persistence*.

Persistence is one of the most important elements to every success. It will be your persistence that will place you inside the winner's circle. Once you start something, complete what you started. Whenever you encounter the bumpy and tough times in your life, it's only a test to see if you will *give up* or *persist forward*.

Get focused and stay focused. Regardless how many times you get knocked off track, keep your focal point on what you want to achieve. Set your goals. Aim toward your goals. Start moving forward to achieve your goals. When you constantly move in the direction toward your goals, you will continuously place yourself on the highway to achieve them.

THE BEST GIVE THEIR BEST

Vince Lombardi, the NFL Hall of Fame Green Bay Packers head coach, once stated, "There is only one way to succeed in anything, and that is to give it everything." We have heard people call others *great* by saying, "He or she is great." Greatness doesn't just happen by coincidence. The word "Great" was born from the words: GIVE IT ALL YOU GOT!

To become great, you must constantly give your best effort by giving *all* you've got. To standout as the best, you must work on improving yourself every single day. To strengthen your personal greatness, you must continually work on improving the quality of your mind, body, health, habits, actions, and results.

> *"There is only one way to succeed in anything,*
> *and that is to give it everything."*
> –VINCE LOMBARDI

When your goal is to become the best, you will need to have a "mental" meeting with yourself. Within your *mental* meeting, you will need to decide if you will "succeed" or "quit." Losers quit. Champions prevail. Will you *quit* or *prevail*?

To become the best, you must *do* your best. Champions succeed through their persistence to give their best performance. Persistence creates champions. Day in and day out, winners perpetually challenge themselves to surpass their previous accomplishments. It will be your persistence that will bring out the *best* in you. It will be your never-ending persistence that will make you standout as a champion.

As a progress thinker, always give your best performance. Never stop giving your best effort, until you have done your best. When you have done your best, don't stop there. Keep striving to improve yourself, so you can accomplish more in your life. When you give your *best* effort, you will receive the *best* rewards, which will display that you gave your *best* performance.

OPEN THE DOOR TO YOUR HIDDEN TALENTS

There are two types of *winners*: The people who take action to win, and the people who only talk about winning. Which <u>one</u> are you? Remember, *talk* is cheap. *Action* is priceless.

One reason people don't succeed is because they haven't consciously prepared themselves to succeed. To win in life, you must mentally, emotionally, and physically prepare yourself for your forthcoming triumphs. Are you ready to succeed? Honestly, if success came and knocked on your door right now would you be mentally, emotionally, spiritually, and physically dressed for the occasion? If not, you still have some more preparing to do. When your objective is to succeed, you will need to be ready for whatever life decides to present to you.

Another reason countless people don't succeed is because they are always *waiting* for the doors to automatically open for them. Instead of opening or building our own doors to succeed, many of us *wait* for someone else to build it or open it for us. Then, there are a few people who don't succeed, simply because they want a free handout. Many people keep themselves from succeeding because they are always waiting to ride someone else's coattail. Although we are living in the 21st century and this is the technological age, have we grown to the point where we want others to do *all* the work for us? Think about it. You could delegate all of your work, but delegating takes work too.

Successful people custom-design their own doors to succeed. One of the most effective ways to prevail is by creating your own success doors. As a progress thinker, start designing your own success doors to walk through. You will succeed, once you stop hiding your unique talents behind closed doors. For example, when you neglect to take action and use your talent, you are hiding your talents. Whenever you hide your talents, you will keep yourself from succeeding. To succeed, you must reveal your talents. Start displaying your unique talents where they can be seen. Once you start implementing your talents, you will begin designing the doors to your own success.

CHAMPIONS PREPARE THEMSELVES

Success starts with *preparation*. The more *prepared* you are to succeed; the farther you will elevate yourself from failure. The retired U.S. Army General and former Secretary of State, Colin Powell once declared, "There are no secrets to success. It is the result of preparation, hard work and learning from failure."

It will be your *preparation* and *persistence* that will produce your success. Progress thinkers become champions because they *prepare* and condition themselves to win. Champions always do whatever it takes to succeed. Are you willing to do whatever it takes? When you fully *prepare* yourself, you will do whatever it takes to show how *prepared* you are by going the extra mile. Let your preparation and persistence speak for you.

To become "the best" you must work harder and more creative than the people who are already *the best*. Here is a helpful hint: You must not only "prepare" yourself *like* the best, you must "prepare" yourself to *go beyond* the best.

> *"Preparation is the doorbell for success.*
> *Persistence is the key to success."*

As Ignas Bernstein asserted, "Do what you know best; if you're a runner, run. If you're a bell, ring." Preparation is the doorbell for success. Persistence is the key to success. When you come across a doorbell that is broken and your goal is to succeed, start knocking on the door. Even if *success* is inside sleeping, keep knocking until success lets you inside. It will be your persistence that will open the doors for you to succeed.

Champions always *prepare* themselves. Start preparing yourself to win like a champion. Think like a champion. Read the books champions read. Meet other champions. Take the action steps that will make you a champion.

KEEP PRESSING FORWARD

As Calvin Coolidge, the 30th President of the Untied States, once stated, "Nothing in the world can take the place of persistence. Talent will not... Genius will not... Education will not... Persistence and determination alone are omnipotent. The slogan 'Press on' has solved and always will solve the problems of the human race."

Successful people know one of the most effective ways to make progress is to *keep pressing on*. To succeed in anything, you must *keep pressing forward*. For example, when it comes to advancing your progress to the next level, losing weight, building your wealth, and/or fast tracking your success the key is to *keep pressing forward*, until you successful achieve your goals.

There are countless people who have encountered stumbling blocks in their lives. Nevertheless, they continued to press onward. When you encounter stumbling blocks, remember, you can knock down the gloomy walls in your life, which will enable you to see brighter days.

One way you can press forward is by stretching your potential. Don't ball up your *potential* and place it at the bottom of your life closet. Pull your *potential* out and *stretch it*. In other words, the more you challenge yourself, the more you will *stretch* yourself to grow into a better, stronger, and persistent person.

Simply sprinkling a little action on top of your beliefs will make a big difference in your results. When your vision is big *enough*, your beliefs are strong *enough*, your determination is focused *enough*, and your actions are moving in forward motion you will have more than *enough* to succeed. You have more than enough potential within you to advance your life to extraordinary levels. You are the only person who knows exactly what level you want to hoist your life and success to. What actions will you take today that will elevate you to the next level?

DREAM & LIVE YOUR DREAMS

Are you *living* your dreams or are you *sitting on* your dreams? You always have a choice about how you will live your own dreams.

Your dreams are unique because they are yours. Are you perpetually taking action toward your dreams or have you just given up on your dreams? If you give up on your dreams, you will keep yourself from fulfilling your dreams. Don't quit or give up on your dreams. Keep moving forward. When you take action to achieve your dreams, you will eventually fulfill your dreams. What action will you take to fulfill and live your *own* dreams today?

ON THE ROAD CALLED SUCCESS

Once you find the road you have been looking for all your life, you will do whatever it takes to stay on that road for the rest of your life. Whatever you want to achieve in your life, you can achieve it. The key is to find the right road to travel on. The road to success is bright, when you discover the right road to travel on.

> *"Once you find the road you have been looking for*
> *all your life, you will do whatever it takes*
> *to stay on that road for the rest of your life."*

Every road toward success usually encounters rough terrain and various roadblocks, such as detours, under construction and wrong way signs that will attempt to deter you from succeeding. As a progress thinker, there will be plenty of obstacles placed on your path that will attempt to derail you from succeeding. Despite the amount of obstacles–negative thinking people, places, and things that will be displayed on your journey, *keep moving forward.* To succeed, you must keep your mind, action, and persistence focused on what you want to achieve. Once you place your persistence, mind, and action in the direction toward what you want to achieve, you will be on *the right road* to achieve it.

When you are on the road toward success: Your...

- *Game Plan* will be your GPS.
- *Action* will be your vehicle.
- *Faith* will be your seatbelt.
- *Determination* will be your steering wheel.
- *Enthusiasm* will be your engine.
- *Persistence* will be your fuel.
- *Success* will be your destination.

When you feel like you want to stop, quit, or give up reread the previous "When you are on the road toward success..." Write it down. Review it. Use it as your daily guide.

When you are the designated driver of your own life, you are in control of your destiny. Stop riding in the passenger seat of someone else's life. Grab your *own* keys and steering wheel. Sit in the driver seat of your *own* life and start driving your *own* life.

CONDITION YOURSELF TO GO THE EXTRA MILE

When I was in the U.S. Marine Corps (USMC), I was taught how to maximize my mind, body, and time productively. Our days usually started very early in the morning, which in military terminology, it's called "O-dark thirty." In the civilian world, it's called "the wee hours of the morning." This particular time frame is usually before the sunrise, when it's dark outside and most people are still in the bed sleeping.

> *"Everyday you have to test yourself.*
> *If not, it's a wasted day."*
> –U.S. MARINE CORPS

It was during my military days when I learned how to mentally, emotionally, and physically push myself beyond limits. The military training that I received taught me how to exceed what my mind *temporarily* believed was impossible. The Marine Corps phrase for this method is called, "Mind Over Matter." For example, let's say you're striving to achieve a goal and suddenly a negative thought enters your mind what would you do? Would you *listen to* the negative bully in your mind? Or, would you *conquer* the negative bully in your mind? You can transform the negative thoughts that enter into your mind. How? By mentally telling yourself, "It doesn't matter because it's only *temporary*." You can also use this strategy when you're exercising.

In Chapter 15, we talked about temporary defeats. When you place your mind over the *temporary* matter, you will begin to condition your mind, actions, and results to go beyond the temporary matter. The USMC standards for mental, emotional, and physical conditioning taught me how go *beyond* an inch or a yard. They taught me how to *go the extra mile*. Though I'm no longer in the Marine Corps, I can still hear my platoon calling out cadences, as we jogged various miles, "One mile...no sweat." "Two miles...no sweat." "Five miles...no sweat."

You don't have to be in the military to go the extra mile. The secret for going the extra mile is to condition yourself mentally, emotionally, and physically to go the extra mile. When you use the words, "I Can," "I Will," and "I Must" you will continuously empower yourself to go the extra mile. Going the extra mile will advance you to the next level. Going the extra mile will make you stand out from the crowd. Going the extra mile will place you across the achievement lines. While others are taking half steps; take a whole step. While others are stopping an inch short; go the extra inch. When you go the extra mile, you will become unstoppable.

As a progress thinker, go the extra mile. As the saying goes in the USMC, "Everyday you have to test yourself. If not, it's a wasted day."

Don't waste your *life* away by wasting your *time* away. Use your time and life more productively. You can do more with your life by challenging yourself every day. Starting today, make every day your best day...Go The Extra Mile!

PERSISTENCE WILL MAKE THE DIFFERENCE

Progress thinkers use their perseverance to succeed. When you condition yourself to keep moving forward and upward, not only will you become persistent, you will also advance your success.

On various occasions, people have asked me, "How can some people succeed, while others don't succeed?" The distinction between *successful* and *unsuccessful* people: Unsuccessful people give up *before* they succeed. Successful people keep going, *until* they succeed. Once you start the momentum toward what you want to achieve, the key is to keep moving forward, *until* you achieve it. Your forward progress will continuously place you across the achievement lines in your life. When you keep moving forward, your persistence will reward you at the end.

TAKE A MOMENT TO PAUSE

When your mind and body starts aching, and you're low on fuel don't quit or throw in the towel. It's only an indication that you need to *take a moment to pause* in your life.

When you get tired, take a moment to catch your second wind. Once you have your second wind, keep pushing yourself forward until you succeed. There will be times in your life when you will need to pause for a moment, so you can get your thoughts together. Once you gather your thoughts together, continue to charge forward on your journey. Remember, when you keep your mind, action, and persistence moving forward in the direction toward your goals, you will arrive at your destination by achieving your goals.

JUST A LITTLE MORE

The wealthy and successful businessman H. Ross Perot once said, "Most people give up just when they're about to achieve success. They quit on the one-yard line. They give up at the last minute of the game one foot from a winning touchdown."

One evening, a family was watching a program on television. During a commercial break, the father noticed a phone number that was displayed on the TV screen. The next day, the father called the phone number. The number was to their local cable company, because he wanted to upgrade their cable channels.

The father went to the cable company and retrieved the new cable box with the extended channels. After arriving home, he quickly pulled everything out of the box and read the instructions. He plugged in all the wires exactly as the instructions indicated. Excited about watching the new channels, he quickly turned on the TV. As he flipped through the channels, he noticed the TV didn't display a foreseeable picture for him to see the new cable channels, so he reread the instructions step-by-step. As he attempted to connect the new cable box again, he was unsuccessful in watching the new channels. He picked up the phone, called the cable company and stated, "The cable box you gave me doesn't work."

The next day, the cable company sent a professional repairman out to check the new cable box. The repairman turned on the TV to see what was wrong with the cable box. He turned the TV off. In a calm manner, the repairman reached behind the TV and turned the cable wire a little. Then, he turned the TV back on. After the repairman turned on the TV, he used the remote control and started flipping through the channels. Amazed that the cable box was working, the father inquired, "What did you do to fix it?" The repairman replied, "All I did was tightened the wire on the back of your TV a little bit because it wasn't screwed all the way into your TV."

The previous scenario happens, on a daily basis. For instance, how many people do you know that give up *before* they succeed in their lives? We all know someone, at least one person or a few people, who gave up *before* they physically succeeded.

Giving up or *going the extra mile* is the barrier that separates success from failure. Progress thinkers succeed because they refuse to give up. They challenge themselves to go the extra mile. How do high achievers challenge themselves? They constantly give their best effort, *until* they cross their own achievement line.

As a progress thinker, keep thriving to cross your *own* achievement line. To achieve your goals, you must go across the *starting* line. Stop waiting behind the starting line of achievement. Start moving toward what you want to achieve. Once you cross the *starting* line, you will start the momentum for you to cross your own *achievement* line.

The key to achievement is to start taking action toward the goals you want to achieve. When you go beyond *who you used to be* and move toward *who you want to be*, you will continually make successful progress in your finances, career, relationships, and endeavors. The more you mentally and physically go for what you want to achieve, the faster you will achieve what you want in your life.

When your objective is to achieve your goals, don't stop in the midst of *achieving* your goals. Keep going, until you *achieve* your goals. In other words, once you start a task, keep going, *until* you complete the task in front of you.

PERSISTENCE CREATE ACHIEVEMENTS

Two of the most vigorous ways to reach your destiny is to *start the process* and *keep moving forward,* Regardless what may happen along the way, keep moving forward.

> *"Although it may not be in the dictionary,*
> *persistence is the definition of success,*
> *because without persistence there is no success."*

The word "persistence" is more than just a word in the dictionary. Although it may not be in the dictionary, *persistence* is the definition of success, because without persistence there is no success. Persistence breeds success. Success comes from persistence. Persistence is about doing whatever it takes to succeed. When it comes to persistence, you must believe you will succeed.

Persistence is about pulling and pushing yourself to keep moving forward, even when you're tired. Persistence is about jumping over the hurdles of fear and overcoming adversities. Persistence is about working harder, more creative, and longer hours to succeed. When it comes to losing weight, persistence is about pushing yourself to exercise and eat healthy foods.

There are many extraordinary things you can accomplish, once you take physical action toward what you want to achieve. When your focal point, enthusiasm, determination, physical action, and persistence are all present and pointing in the same direction, you will continuously cross the achievement line to succeed in your life.

UNSTOPPABLE GAME PLAN

Benjamin Franklin once stated, "Energy and persistence conquer all things." When you become enthusiastic and persistent about what you want to accomplish, you become *unstoppable*.

Like a locomotive train, once you connect your *vision* (what you want to achieve) with your *passion*, *physical action* and *persistence* you will become UNSTOPPABLE!

Start your day with a game plan. Develop a game plan that will make you unstoppable! Get enthusiastic about your game plan. Start taking action to achieve your game plan. A game plan is <u>not</u> successful until the game plan has been successfully accomplished. The more you accomplish, the more you will become unstoppable.

Make every day an *unstoppable* day! When naysayers attempt to stop you, keep moving forward. You will become unstoppable, once you become a *go-forward* person. Whatever challenges you experience–good or bad–continue to *go-forward*. To succeed, you must *go-forward*. When you continue to move forward, in the direction toward your goals and dreams, your momentum will accelerate you across the achievement line.

THE GAME CALLED FORWARD THINKING

The following technique is what I call *Forward Thinking*. The advantage to forward thinking is that you can *mentally* design your forthcoming results, *before* you physically produce the results.

In short-term, *forward thinking* is a mental preview of your forthcoming success. Forward thinking is a *pre-vision*. A pre-vision is a mental visualization of what you want to achieve *before* you physically achieve it. The key to forward thinking is to *think ahead*. For example, Tiger Woods, the professional golfer, uses the forward thinking technique. When Tiger Woods plays golf, he mentally visualizes the game. Have you ever noticed how Tiger Woods approaches the tee? Tiger takes a moment to *mentally* visualize how he will hit his golf ball into the hole, <u>before</u> he *physically* hits the ball into the hole. That's *forward thinking*.

As I like to say, "it's good to get in the game. However, it's outstanding to stay ahead of the game." Stay in front of the game. Don't wait for the game to begin. Mentally and physically stay in front of your goals. Start thinking forward in your life. Imagine yourself *physically* achieving your forthcoming goals. To win, you must *stay ahead of the game*, not behind the game.

When you want better results, use the *forward thinking* technique. Mentally see yourself succeeding in advance. You can also use *forward thinking* for your goals. For instance, as you're writing down your goals, think five, ten, and twenty years ahead. When you use *forward thinking* it will enable you to think, win, and achieve your goals faster. When you *think forward*, you will begin to move forward. When you *move forward*, you will begin to make forward progress.

YOU ARE A WINNER

There is always a way to win. The two key questions you must personally ask and answer: First, what do you want to win? Second, how bad do you want to win? There are no rules or laws that states, "Every winner must be an athlete, extremely wealthy, or have the picture perfect body to be classified as a winner." Regardless of what you have seen, heard, and/or been through in your life–you have what it takes to win.

> *"There is always a way to win. The two key questions you must personally ask and answer: First, what do you want to win? Second, how bad do you want to win?"*

As a progress thinker, you create the game plan for your own life and success. You will achieve more once you develop a game plan to win. To become a winner, you will need to think like a winner. To win, you will need to think progress and take physical action. To succeed, you will need to think in an optimistic manner, instead of in a pessimistic manner. To conquer, you will need to believe that you *can and will* win. To prevail, you will need to set and achieve goals.

You are the only person who knows the exact destination that you want to arrive at in your life. Develop your game plan, and begin to take action toward your game plan, before you know it you will successfully arrive at your destination as a winner.

YOU CAN...

If you can think it, you can do it.

If you can believe it, you can conquer it.

If you want it bad enough, you can get it.

If you take action, you can achieve it.

YOU CAN SUCCEED!

–SKIP J. WILLIAMS

THINK PROGRESS DAILY A – Z CHECKLIST

A = Always strive to improve yourself daily.

B = Believe in yourself and build your own success mountain.

C = Commit yourself to what you want to achieve.

D = Do tasks that will enable you to succeed.

E = Everyday is a brand new day to advance your progress.

F = Forward thinking will display your forthcoming success.

G = Give yourself the permission to achieve more in your life.

H = Happiness and success are both reachable destinations.

I = "I will have an outstanding day no matter what happens."

J = Jot down what you want to achieve in your life.

K = Keep moving forward until you succeed.

L = Let your actions and results do all the talking for you.

M = Maximize your actions and game plan daily.

N = Never say "I give up," "I quit" or "I can't."

O = Open your mind to new ideas.

P = Push your envelope to the next level.

Q = Quality time is a necessity for quality results.

R = Results will make the difference in your progress.

S = Set new standards for yourself to achieve.

T = Take action to achieve your dreams and goals.

U = Unleash your internal risk taker.

V = Visualize yourself accomplishing your excitements (goals).

W = Wake up your mental vision and physically live it.

X = X marks the spot where you are located in your life.

Y = You will succeed when you keep giving your best performance.

Z = Zoom in and focus on achieving your dreams and goals.

POSTSCRIPT

As an author, it's rewarding to receive feedback from the readers. If you have any comments that you would like to share, I would love to hear from you. While reading *Think Progress*, did a particular story, quote, or strategy inspire you? What life-changing lessons did you learn? How have you applied what you learned? How did *Think Progress* help you? Every day you have the opportunity to reach for new and higher levels— reach for the stars.

Your success matters to me. At Skip Williams Communications LLC, the ultimate goal is to help *you* succeed. This is the core reason why I continue to push myself and burn the midnight oil, even in the daytime, because I want to help you achieve your dreams and goals. Every day I work around the clock seeking, discovering, developing, and revealing the world's best strategies that will enhance and maximize the quality of your life, performance, results, and success.

For more information about products, services, and forthcoming events, or if you would like to inquire about my availability as a speaker for your next event, you can contact me via:

Skip Williams Communications LLC
P.O. Box 7071, New York, NY 10116

Phone: 646-580-8405
E-mail: skip@skipwilliamsonline.com
www.skipwilliamsonline.com

164

ABOUT THE AUTHOR

Skip J. Williams is an author, professional speaker, and entrepreneur. Mr. Williams is the founder and CEO of Skip Williams Communications LLC, a personal and professional development firm specializing in leadership, entrepreneurship, peak performance, and executive coaching. Skip is also known as "The Next Level Coach," due to his never-ending commitment to elevate his clients and audiences to the next level. His exceptional life-changing strategies for personal and professional success continues to challenge, inspire, and transform more achievers each year, as his audience continues to broaden to new arenas. Skip has served in the United States Marine Corps. He has stood in front and behind the camera, as the executive producer and host of his own self-help TV show called *The Skip Williams Show*. He is the creative author of *Think & Win Big*. He lives in New York City.

www.ingramcontent.com/pod-product-compliance
Lightning Source LLC
Chambersburg PA
CBHW031512040426
42445CB00009B/200